To Jim & Cindy
Travel far, ride sy—
& eat well!

# LISA'S RIDDEN ROUTE
## A GLOBAL KITCHEN

Spanish Chicken

Pineapple Prawn Picks

Simon's Tummato Sauce

Asado

Cheap Chili Con Carne

**Lisa has prepared and cooked delicious meals in 78 countries on 6 continents.**

Mongolian Make-Do Stew

Couscous

Orange Pork

Thai green Curry

DEPARTURE
Aeropuerto
BARCELONA
2...10.2012
Reid...

ALIA
...GRATION
SYDNEY

# ADVANCE PRAISE

*"I'm a passionate traveller and cookbook collector and Lisa has nailed it. This is one of the best cookbooks I've seen in ages, not just for overlanders and especially adventure riders but for anyone who loves food and travel. The thoughtfully chosen and carefully tested recipes are introduced by short vignettes of the region or trip-event that inspired them, making you want to jump on a bike immediately and head to far-off places. Add to the stories and recipes the gorgeous images and beautiful layout and you have the perfect recipe for a really top-notch reader- and diner-experience. I suspect this book will soon become one of the 'must-haves' for any overlander's library."*
   —Roseann Hanson, Founder and Owner, Overland Expo

*"Eating healthy on the road is often more of a challenge than the ride itself! Lisa Thomas knows better than anyone how to whip up a great meal in the middle of nowhere, from limited or frankly peculiar ingredients, using just the few utensils that can be carried on a motorcycle. This book will inspire you to avoid the gas station snacks and become an adventure gourmet."*
   —Lois Pryce, Author, *Lois on the Loose*

*"Visually stunning, this book is packed with hard-earned experience, top healthy eating tips, fun, mouthwatering recipes so good you'll want to be using them at home, too."*
   —Sam Manicom, Motorcycle Overlander, Author, and Travel Writer

*"With this sharing of worldly condiments and delectable ingredients, we find ourselves getting lost in Lisa's mesmerizing stories and recipes as we join her on this magic carpet ride that sews cultures together into a tapestry of the most scrumptious feast for both the mouth and heart."*
   —Nicole Espinosa, *Adventure Motorcycle Magazine*

*"If you are not fortunate enough to be able to enjoy Lisa's cooking skills firsthand, you can sample these recipes for yourself, and perhaps dream of far-flung lands."*
   —Cory Friend, Travel Director and Food Snob

"*Lisa is hands down the Julia Child of the adventure motorcycle world.*"
   —Luanna Van Holten, Black Swan Moto

"*Lisa's Thai Curry is simply the best I've ever eaten!*"
   —Ted Simon, Author, *Jupiter's Travels*

"*Lisa's ability to think outside the pannier when it comes to sourcing and making great food on the road will be a tremendous skill for you, whether you are in your own backyard or halfway to nowhere.*"
   —Amie Bailey, Chef/Owner, Earlybird Cafe, San Francisco, California

"*Lisa has a talent of transforming everyday ingredients into mouthwatering dishes. I was an okay cook, however, not very imaginative in the kitchen until I met Lisa. She has inspired me by her love of cooking to try different recipes from different cultures and discover a whole new level and enjoyment to cooking. I know this book will do the same for you.*"
   —Jacqui Powell, longtime friend and business partner

"*Cooking on a stove, with few ingredients, after a day's riding through God knows what conditions is not an easy job. Still, eating at "Lisa's" is a five star experience. I don't know how she does it, but I was left with the impression that she can cook out of nothing. Surely, being so many years on the road is her best ingredient. There's no other person I could think of that I would ask advice from when it comes to cooking while travelling. Ever since Lisa mentioned the idea of writing a book on her travel cooking experience, I reserved some room in my bike's tank bag.*"
   —Mihai Barbu, Traveller and Author of *Vand Kilometri*

"*While waiting for the first of many of Lisa's meals I remember smelling the first waft of spicy aromas emitting from an adjacent room. All I could think about was tasting the first mouthfuls of this incredible smelling meal. As I entered the room where Lisa was cooking I couldn't believe what she was preparing, solely from two small camp pots. The end result was remarkable.*"
   —Peter Domhill, World Traveller

# FOR THE THREE MOST IMPORTANT PEOPLE IN MY LIFE

For my mother and late father.
Thank you for all of the travelling, camping, and
camp cooking we did as a family during my early
years. Those wonderful times helped me become
the adventurer I am today.

For my very patient husband Simon.
He has been a wonderful guinea pig trying out
these recipes time and time again in some of the
most remote parts of this wonderful planet.
I haven't managed to poison him so far.

# DIRTY DINING
## AN ADVENTURER'S COOKBOOK

LISA THOMAS

LIONESS PRESS
Hendersonville, NC

Lioness Press books may be purchased for educational, business, or sales promotional use. For information, please email the Special Markets Department at info@lionesspress.us.

Design, layout, and photography by Simon Thomas
Edited by Williamaye Anne Jones

FIRST EDITION
Printed in the United States of America
ISBN 978-0-692-05831-2
10 9 8 7 6 5 4 3 2 1

# MY MOTHER HAS ALWAYS BEEN A SOURCE OF INSPIRATION

My mother has always been a source of inspiration when it comes to preparing meals. During my childhood years she fed us with a huge variety of cuisines, ranging from Italian pasta dishes, Thai stir-frys, traditional British roasts, and South African stews. I was an eclectic eater from a very young age.

I first started cooking at the age of twelve, in my home economics lessons in school, and an enjoyment for cooking and feeding people continued to grow. So, when I first sat down to write this book I thought, "Simple! I love to cook, this will be a breeze!"

How wrong could I have been?

During the development of this book, and much to Simon's delight, I cooked many of my recipes over and over again. As is often the case with food, each meal returned vivid and beautiful memories of the stunning and sometimes challenging landscapes we've traveled during our fourteen-year journey.

I'm not sure that a cookbook can have, or is meant to have, a message but if there is one it's this:

Whether you are restricted by time, money, supplies, or all three, you do not need to live on noodles and tuna alone!

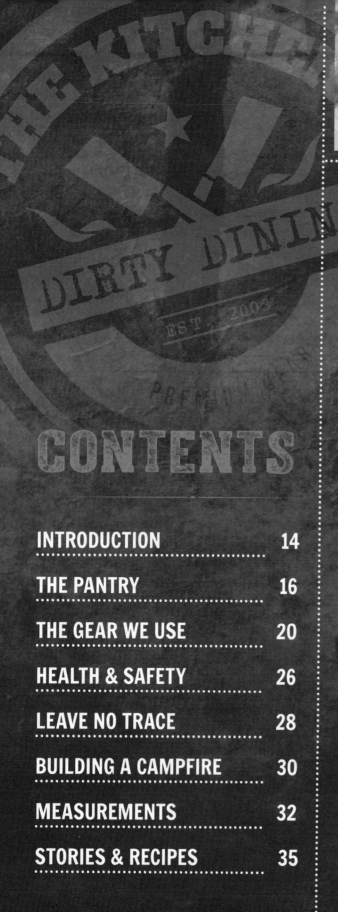

# CONTENTS

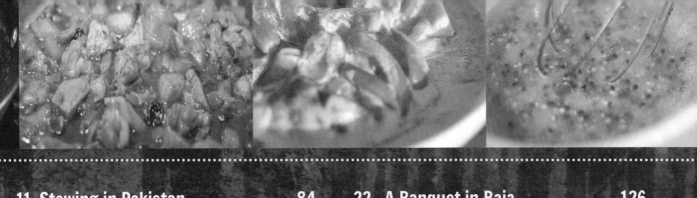

# INTRODUCTION

**L**uckily for Simon, I love to cook, and I like to think that our mutual love of food is just one of the reasons our relationship is still strong today. I love to cook, Simon loves to eat: it's a simple but great partnership. If I remember correctly, our first "date" included me cooking for him at three in the morning.

After more than fourteen years on the road, I still enjoy the challenges that feeding both of us entails. I love to wander through local markets and marvel at the exotic, intoxicating and often-unrecognizable ingredients. I adore the smell of the spices in the markets of Morocco and India, the variety and intense flavour of the meats in Argentina and, my favourite, the glorious markets and street food stalls of Asia.

Food is one of the greatest pleasures of travel. But why cook when you can enjoy the local foods and experience the culture of the country you are travelling through? There are times when food is scarce, when there are no markets, restaurants or food stalls. What do you do then?

> ### THIS BOOK IS NOT INTENDED TO BE A GOURMET COOKING GUIDE OR EVEN A COUNTRY-BY-COUNTRY RECIPE BOOK.

This book is not intended to be a gourmet cooking guide or even a country-by-country recipe book—that one's still in the works and will be published later. This book gets down to the nitty-gritty of how to make do when there is nothing much around to eat. The recipes in this book are for when you are out in the "boonies" where fresh produce is scarce to nonexistent, or high up in the Altiplano riding at 15,000 feet. Maybe you're in the desert at 122°F (50°C) or struggling in the sodden tundra fighting elephant-sized mosquitoes. Or perhaps you are just too plain broke and tired to engage your imagination and work out what the hell to do with that tin of tuna and other basic items that you have with you.

I want to share with you the lessons I've learned from my time travelling the world, and from my background as a health and fitness professional. I want to show you how, with just a small selection of basic foodstuffs, it is possible to produce quick, tasty, and nutritious meals.

Remember, too, that your diet needs to be varied and combined in a way that gives you the best chance of absorbing as many nutrients as possible. Maintaining a healthy diet can be near impossible when travelling through developing parts of the world, where fresh vegetables are nowhere to be seen. No one food contains everything you need for optimum nourishment, and a day riding off-road can be brutal and leave you physically drained. At the end of each hard day your body is screaming out to be refuelled but, to refuel, you'll need to actually want to eat the meal you've prepared, so make it a good one.

It's easy to get by on snacking and eating out of tins, relying on tuna and noodles, but if you plan to be on the road any longer than three to four weeks, you will need to be better prepared.

The recipes in this book are based on real-world recipes. Each one takes into account that you'll be replenishing your food stock out on the road and that you won't have a deli close at hand. None of my recipes require you to prepare ingredients before you leave or utilize ingredients that need refrigeration. I don't carry a refrigerator on my travels, and I'm guessing you won't, either.

Any recipes that contain meat assumes that you will buy the meat or poultry on the day it will be cooked. Just remember to purchase it in the afternoon rather than first thing in the morning. Meat slowly baking in the day's heat whilst you ride is a great way to lose a lot of weight via food poisoning.

It's easy to carry fresh vegetables and fruit with you for a few days whilst on the road, but be aware of how you store these if you are wild camping as you don't want to attract animals. Root vegetables such as potatoes, yams, sweet potatoes, onions, and carrots will last much longer without bruising or going mouldy. Vegetables such as zucchini, tomatoes, green beans, and peppers, should last a couple of days in most climates. The idea is to buy fresh when you can and use it on the day of purchase.

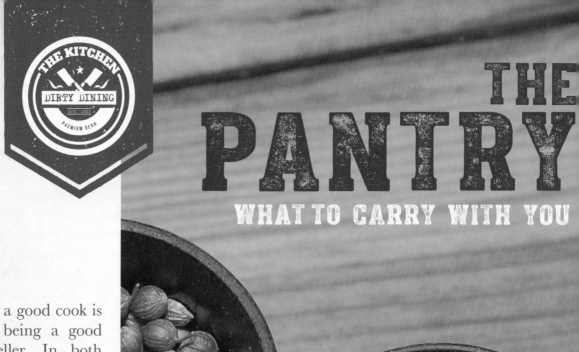

# THE PANTRY

## WHAT TO CARRY WITH YOU

**B**eing a good cook is like being a good traveller. In both cases, the ability to be flexible is crucial.

I try to keep the same basic ingredients with me wherever we travel in the world. If I can't find exactly what I need, a substitute will always do. From experience, I know that the majority of items in this list are easy to locate almost anywhere in the world.

LISA THOMAS

## › DRIED HERBS
### SECRET INGREDIENT

- Curry powder
- Mixed herbs
- Paprika
- Ginger
- Cayenne pepper
- Cinnamon
- Coriander seeds
- Dried chilli
- Cumin
- Salt
- Pepper

## › FLAVOURS
### BIG ON TASTE

- Worcestershire sauce
- Soy sauce
- Olive oil
- Tabasco (or other hot sauce)
- Honey
- Sesame oil
- If you are unable to find small bottles make sure you decant into small plastic (leak-proof) containers.

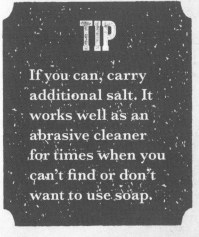

**TIP**

If you can, carry additional salt. It works well as an abrasive cleaner for times when you can't find or don't want to use soap.

## › PACKETS
### SAVING THE DAY

- Soup packets
- Green curry paste
- Taco/chilli seasoning (If you prefer you can mix your own from the spices you carry but often, for speed, I use a packet if I have been able to find one.)
- Brown gravy
- Rice seasoning (If you have the chance to head into a Chinese or Thai supermarket these packets are a great time-saver.)
- Dried peas
- Concentrated tomato puree

## › SMALL TINS
### TRAVEL PANTRY

- Spam
- Tuna
- Mixed vegetable (Usually contains a mix of chopped pieces of potato, carrot, and peas, which can add both flavour and additional colour to a meal.)
- Corn
- Mushroom

## › PRODUCTS
ESSENTIALS

- Pasta
- Rice
- Couscous
- Powdered milk
- Coffee
- Tea bags
- Sugar/sweetener
- Stock cubes (Variety if possible of beef, chicken, vegetable, and fish.)
- Corn flour, aka corn starch (An essential ingredient for thickening stews and sauces.)

> **TIP**
>
> Spaghetti is easier to pack than shells or shaped pasta.

## COOKING GEAR

## KITCHEN GEAR

## FOOD PREP GEAR

## SERVING GEAR

## WEAPONARY

## UTENSILS

# THE GEAR WE USE

**THE KITCHEN**

**DIRTY DINING**

EST. 2003

PREMIUM GEAR

**A**ll of the items listed in both kitchen equipment and foodstuffs are easily packed into one pannier with space to spare. Of course, if you're travelling solo, you will carry less anyway, though it's nice to double up on a few things so you can share. If you're riding two-up you have to be a lot more selective and will choose only absolutely essential items.

# › COOKING GEAR
## COME ON BABY LIGHT MY FIRE

- 1 MSR Dragonfly stove
- 1 MSR 11 oz. fuel bottle
- 1 MSR Expedition service kit
- 1 grill rack (essential for cooking on an open fire)

# › FOOD PREP GEAR
## WHERE IT ALL STARTS

- 1 vegetable peeler
- MSR folding chopping board
- Pannier-sized thin chopping board
  (Slides inside of a pannier.)

# › KITCHEN GEAR
## THIS IS THE GEAR YOU USE TO COOK IN

- Small frying pan (I prefer not to use the camping variety but use a small 7" nonstick frying pan. I have only had to buy two during our eleven years on the road. They last a long time!)
- A 2 litre, two saucepan, nesting kit
- 4 egg poacher "pouches"
- 6 metal skewers (Essential for cooking on an open fire.)

# WEAPONRY
## THE STUFF YOU EAT WITH

- 2 MSR Alpine Kitchen Knives
- 2 MSR titanium spoons
- 2 MSR titanium forks
- 2 teaspoons
- 2 pairs of chopsticks (It's a real treat for us to carry these, as they were a gift from friends in Japan.)

# SERVING GEAR
## THE STUFF YOU EAT OUT OF

- 2 MSR Alpine stainless-steel bowls
- 2 MSR Alpine stainless-steel plates
- 3 titanium stackable mugs (One spare for a visitor.)
- 2 stainless-steel tumblers (This is a luxury as I got fed up with drinking absolutely everything from a mug as the years passed.)
- 2 small tin saucers (From our time in India, and great containers for a side of salsa or other condiments.)

# UTENSILS
## THE STUFF THAT MAKES LIFE EASIER

- A few sheets of tin foil (Essential for cooking on an open fire.)
- 1 can opener
- 1 mini Norton knife sharpener stone
- 1 small wooden spoon (Yes, I'm old-fashioned.)
- 1 small wooden spatula
- 1 MSR folding spatula
- 1 MSR pan handler
- Clothes pegs (For clipping bags closed.)
- 1 small plastic bottle (Great for mixing a dressing.)
- 1 small grater (For grating cinnamon into hot chocolate or grating lemon zest.)
- Zip-top bags

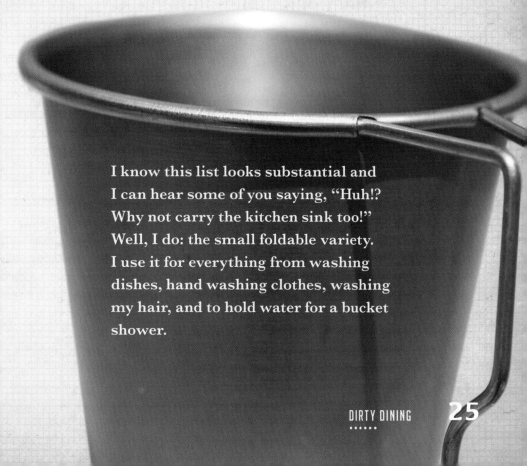

I know this list looks substantial and I can hear some of you saying, "Huh!? Why not carry the kitchen sink too!" Well, I do: the small foldable variety. I use it for everything from washing dishes, hand washing clothes, washing my hair, and to hold water for a bucket shower.

# HEALTH & SAFETY

**Travelling for a long time in countries not our own, we realize that we are often far from medical services, so we keep ourselves as fit and healthy as we possibly can. We also take care to respect the earth we live on and the societies we visit by keeping the sites we camp on neat and clean.**

Whilst on the road, Simon and I have only ever become ill from bad food when I haven't cooked it. (The treat of dining in a restaurant has occasionally turned out not to be a treat at all.) Fact is, most people infect themselves because they haven't followed basic food safety practices. Almost all food poisoning takes eight hours to three days to manifest. I will cover keeping fit and healthy on the road in another book, but I want to point out a few of my golden rules to avoid making yourself sick.

**1** Wash your hands before preparing food and eating. Use soap and rinse well.

**2** If water is scarce, use an antibacterial hand wash or wet wipes.

**3** To be sure water (other than bottled) is safe to drink and use, boil it, treat it or filter it. Simon and I carry an MSR gravity fed water filtration system.

**4** Wash fruit and vegetables using clean running water or water that you are sure is clean. Use bottled or treated water. If there isn't much water around, add a few drops of antibacterial solution such as "macrobiotic" or use a wet-wipe. Then dry them in direct sunlight to help sanitize them. Salt is also a great abrasive cleaner for times when you can't find soap.

**5** Make sure any bottled water you purchase has an unbroken seal.

**6** Clean your chopping board, food preparation areas (especially in hostels), and kitchenware with soap and "safe" water, and let dry completely before reuse.

**7** Cook food well. Keep it covered and eat it hot.

**8** The danger zone for food storage is 40–140 degrees Fahrenheit. If your food has been stored between these temperatures for longer than four hours, make sure you heat it to boiling before eating.

**9** A dirty towel is full of bacteria, so don't use a dirty towel to dry you hands or your plates and utensils.

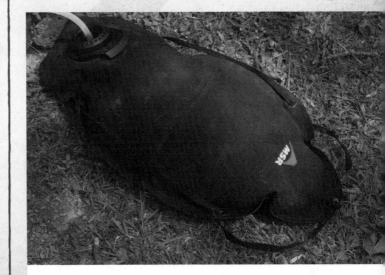

## THE LEAVE NO TRACE RULE

# LNT

### TRAVEL SMART

★ 2RTW ★

We've spent nights in campsites that have listed so many rules and regulations that we've been afraid to even set foot outside our tent for fear of being in the wrong. But often, especially in developing countries, you are left to your own devices. Here, more than anywhere, it is important to follow the principles of Leave No Trace (LNT).

LNT, simply put, is a code of conduct. Basically, it means that whatever you take in with you, you should also take out. Pack out your trash and leave things as you found it (or better than).

Here are some basic rules that we try to follow wherever we camp and cook.

1. Store your food and cooking gear away after every use and keep it clean and free of food odour in order to protect it (and you) from wild animals.

2. Avoid cooking too close to your tent, as the smell may attract animals.

3. Do not store food in your tent. This can be especially dangerous in areas where there are bears and animals who can hurt you in their quest to get to your food.

4. Don't leave packs containing food unattended, even for a few minutes. At one point during our travels I temporarily placed some raw sausages in my pannier case top bag. Later that night I woke up to find four raccoons sitting on my bike having a feast. Luckily nothing had been damaged, ripped, or torn, but we did miss out on a good breakfast.

5. Dispose of your waste water at least 100 feet (30 meters) from a water-course. Do not wash your dishes in lakes, ponds, rivers, or streams unless you are using a biodegradable washing liquid.

6. Do not cook with an open fire near your tent, as embers can burn holes in your flysheet. Build your fires a distance away and down wind. (See the next section on how to build a safe fire.)

7. Treat garbage the same as you would food items.

8. In the USA, all garbage must be carried out of the backcountry, regardless of whether or not you are in a national park. We try to follow this same rule wherever we are. However, there were many times outside of North America when we found it impossible and impractical to follow the LNT rule. For example, in Mali we didn't find a village for days, and Botswana was so incredibly hot that carrying rubbish would have increased our risk of attack from animals during the day. Our solution was to bury it, and sometimes we'd burn it first, before burying.

9. When you set up a garbage burn pit make sure it's located downwind and keep it small.

10. Meat or poultry food waste should also be burned or buried.

11. Crush containers that cannot be burned and then bury them away from your camping area.

12. A note of warning: Be careful to stay upwind of the noxious toxins that may be released when burning materials like plastics, rubber, and Styrofoam.

# BUILDING A CAMPFIRE

## GET IT RIGHT

Before you start building your fire, ensure you know the current fire restrictions in that area. Use existing fire rings if they are available, and check if a campfire permit is required. Simon and I always carry a small shovel and we always make sure that there is a container of water nearby. In North America you will be "held liable for the cost of suppression and damages caused by any wildfire that starts through negligence on your part." Though many countries have no such regulations, it's still important to follow a few basic safety rules.

Simon and I always set our fire pit in a flat, open area at least 15 feet away from anything that may catch fire, including our tent. Look out for overhanging branches, brush, and dry grass.

# BUILDING A SAFE CAMPFIRE

Always clear the area surrounding your fire pit. It's amazing just how far red-hot embers can fly.

We keep our fires small, as they are easier to control and safer. We also want to avoid attention from locals.

Simon collects the firewood whilst I gather small rocks to build a small holding wall for our fire pit. We build the wall so that the rocks are all touching each other. If there are no rocks we pile dirt or sand around the rim.

We never leave our campfire unattended, even for a few minutes. We never let it burn down on its own or bury it under dirt because fires can continue to smoulder for hours. Instead, we drown the fire before we head into our tent for the night and at least 30 minutes before we break camp and head off. This gives us time to make sure that the fire is well and truly out

before we leave the area. I'm a bit of a control freak so I double-check that there is no heat left in the embers and that the fire is actually out and not smouldering.

The bottom line here is that common sense rules. If you're unsure if the spot you found is suitable for a fire, then it's probably best to look somewhere else. If you are setting up in a hurry, in the dark, or are overly tired, simple rules can be missed.

Your fire is your responsibility.

# MEASUREMENTS

## QUANTITIES AND MEASURES

## MEASUREMENTS

Let's face it, not many of you will carry a set of measuring spoons or a measuring jug whilst on the road. So I've tried to make it easy for you by using common utensils and containers.

**1** Tsp. (teaspoon)

**2** Tbsp. (tablespoon) = 3 teaspoons

**3** 1 cup = 16 tablespoons

**4** 240 ml = 1 cup (A can of coke is 330ml, so to measure 1 cup, the can would need to be roughly ¾ full.)

# STORIES & RECIPES

meat

vegetarian

fish

chicken

pasta

eggs

# STORIES & RECIPES

E ach of these recipes is set firmly in a place. But with few adjustments you'll be able to make them anywhere. For example, the fish dish in the first recipe was created in Africa, but I've also made it in Thailand and Mexico. After all, fish, garlic, ginger, lime, and coriander (cilantro), are commonly found in many places. Part of the fun is experimenting with local ingredients to sweeten or spice it up. Got a twist on any of my recipes? I'd love to hear about it. Email me at LisaThomas@2ridetheworld.com.

# 01 | A FISHY TALE IN SENEGAL

**T**he four most gruelling days of our lives was a ride through the largest desert on the planet, the Sahara. Riding the deep sand and towering dunes had pushed us to our limits, and then the relentless heat had pushed us beyond them.

South of the Sahara we pushed on through Mauritania and into the vibrant country of Senegal, where the city of Dakar perches on the northwest African coast.

We were excited to arrive at Lac Rose (The Pink Lake) in time to witness the final stage of the 2004 Paris Dakar Rally.

The days prior had been beautifully quiet. Strolling along the beach amidst a haze of mist from the crashing waves we watched a solitary fisherman stalk the shore, nets in hand, looking for the telltale signs of the shoal's movement.

LISA THOMAS

## IN A FLASH OF AN EYE THE NET WAS CAST AND, BULGING FULL, HAULED TO SHORE.

It seemed rude not to buy at least a few for dinner, so seven still-flapping fish were bought for 3,000 CFA (about £2.80). Okay, we've bought them, but how the hell were we going to carry them? We find a plastic bag (sadly plastic bags pollute every village, town, and shoreline on this coastline) and rinse it in the sea before dropping the reluctant fish inside. We struggle to carry our flapping purchase back to camp. Direct from the sea to your plate ... dinner doesn't get much fresher!

Back at camp, David and Katja in their Land Rover were eagerly waiting. Their excitement was quashed by cries of, "Get that thing away from me!" and "Eewwww! There's no way I can touch that! It's still alive!"

It was obvious they didn't have the stomach for what needed to be done. After calling everyone a few well-chosen names, I set about killing, gutting, and de-scaling. The fish were made ready for the fire whilst Simon and David headed into the small town of Rufisque to buy 16 large beers for 500 CFA (about 50p) each.

The fish were cooked in marinade, on a wire grill over an open fire.

Prep time: 5 minutes
Cooking time: 20 minutes
Utensils: sharp knife, barbeque grill

# GRILLED FISH

## ingredients

» *Fresh fish, preferably red snapper (Approx. 1 lb per person)*

» *1 lime, sliced*

## marinade

» *3 tbsp. olive oil*

» *2 cloves garlic, finely chopped*

» *1 tbsp. ginger, finely chopped*

» *1 tbsp. fresh chilli, finely chopped*

» *2 tbsp. coriander, finely chopped (Stems and leaves.)*

» *½ lime finely zested (The outermost part of the rind, lightly grated.)*

## method

1. Coat your hands with a dollop of olive oil and rub it on the grill thoroughly before cooking. Make sure the fire is not roaring flames but hot embers. We want to cook the fish, not cremate it!

2. To make the marinade, place all ingredients in a bowl and mix well.

3. To descale the fish, lay it flat on its side and scrape it from tail to head on both sides with the dull edge of a knife or edge of a spoon. Hold the fish under water whilst you descale it, the scales will fly everywhere!

4. Rinse and gut the fish. Slice it from the vent on the underbelly upwards and away from the guts towards the head. Make sure you continue up through the bony portion to the base of the lower jaw. Remove the guts by grabbing them right at the base of the head, where you will feel everything connect. Pull the whole lot out. On a larger fish, you'll need a knife to cut the guts out from the base. Make sure you scrape out the liver and all of the swim bladder, which is a whitish sac. Finally, cut out the gills as they create a bitter flavour.

5. Rinse the fish inside and out with clean water.

6. With a sharp knife, score the fish lightly with incisions on both sides approximately 1 cm apart (about the width of the handle of a spoon). This will ensure that the flavour of the marinade penetrates. Trim off the tail and fins so they don't burn.

7. Rub the marinade onto the fish, inside and out.

8. Place a thin layer of lime slices inside the fish.

9. Place the fish on the grill over direct heat, and cook for approximately 10 minutes on each side.

10. You can easily tell when the fish is cooked, as its eyes will be white and protrude slightly.

Early in our trip, we decided to explore Europe. Simon and I had travelled through Spain many times prior to this journey, but we wanted to have one more tour of this wonderfully vibrant country before we left the European continent for what we knew was going to be years.

I first cooked Spanish Chicken in a small campsite on the beach in Tarifa, in the province of Andalusia on the southernmost coast of Spain. We'd camped for weeks waiting for bike parts before crossing the Straits of Gibraltar to head into Africa. This meal soon became a group favourite amongst the eager backpackers and energized kite surfers.

Prep time: 15 minutes (Includes browning the
    chicken pieces.)
Cooking time: 30 minutes
Utensils: 2-litre saucepan

## ingredients

»   500g/1 lb. chicken pieces (Leave the skin on if you're a vegetarian or, if
    you can't find chicken, potatoes cut into large chunks will do.)

»   1 small chorizo sausage, chopped (You can use a processed sausage
    instead of chorizo, although chorizo is fine to carry well-wrapped for a
    few days.)

»   6 medium-sized tomatoes, chopped (I prefer to use plump plum
    tomatoes if I can find them. If you can't find fresh tomatoes, use a
    small tin, instead.)

»   Chopped ham (The equivalent of 5 sandwich-sized slices, or a small tin
    of Spam.)

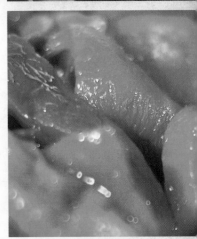

»   Roasted red pepper (see recipe on page 49) cut into long thin strips

»   1 medium red onion, chopped

»   1 chilli pepper chopped (Optional, or use chili flakes.)

»   ½ tsp. of paprika (Less, if you don't like it too spicy.)

»   3 garlic cloves, chopped

»   Pinch of mixed herbs

»   1 tbsp. tomato puree

»   2 tbsp. olive oil

»   175 ml (approx. ¾) cup chicken stock

»   Salt

# SPANISH CHICKEN

Serve with potatoes, rice or fresh bread if you're lucky enough to find some. If you are having this meal with rice, use the recipe on page 77. Cover and leave it to steam and it will remain hot.

Don't worry if the chicken has to wait for your potatoes or rice to finish cooking. As long as you replace the lid the contents will stay hot.

## method

1. Lightly salt the chicken skin (unless you decide to remove the skin prior to cooking) and leave for a few minutes as you prepare the rest of the ingredients.

2. Chop the chorizo and tomatoes into bite-sized pieces.

3. Dice the onion.

4. Slice your pre-prepared roasted red pepper into long, thin strips. (See recipe for roasted red pepper on page 49.)

5. Chop the ham into bite-sized pieces.

6. Skin and chop the garlic.

7. Add 2 tbsp. of olive oil into the pan and heat.

8. Place the chicken skin-side down to brown in the hot olive oil. Once the skin is golden, turn it over to ensure the chicken pieces are browned on both sides. (If you're using potatoes, skip this step.)

9. Put the chicken aside onto a plate before adding it back in step 12.

10. Add the sliced chorizo into the oil and fry for approximately 3 minutes over a medium flame, stirring until the chorizo is browned and the oil starts to run out. (Yum.) Do not let the chorizo burn.

11. Add to the pan with your chorizo the chopped onion, garlic, dried herbs, and chilli. Cook, stirring for 2 minutes to soften the garlic and onion.

12. Add the paprika and return the chicken pieces to the pan. If you're using potatoes, this is where you add them in. Stir well and make sure that all the chicken pieces (or potato) are well coated with the paprika.

13. Add the chopped tomatoes and stir well.

14. Pour in about ¾ of your stock (150ml), saving the remainder in case it becomes too dry. Stir well.

15. Add the tomato puree. (Using puree will make the sauce richer and ensure a delicious consistency.) If the sauce begins to thicken or it becomes too dry, add more of the stock. We are looking for a thick, spoon-coating consistency.

16. Bring the saucepan to a simmer and cover with the lid and cook for 10 minutes, stirring occasionally.

17. After 10 minutes, remove the lid and add the chopped ham and slivers of red pepper in their olive oil. Stir and cook, without the lid, for a further 10 minutes or until your chicken, or potato is thoroughly cooked. If you have substituted chicken for potato, the final 10 minutes of cooking time will be substantially reduced. Just make sure that your potatoes don't totally disintegrate before you serve.

18. Remove from the heat and don't worry if it has to sit and wait for your potatoes or rice to finish cooking. As long as you replace the lid, the contents will stay hot.

ARGENTINIAN FLAVOUR

LISA THOMAS

R ed peppers add flavour to potentially dull meals and are easy to find in most parts of the world. I love cooking them over an open fire alongside a nice juicy steak. This makes a very simple meal and one that we enjoy when on the road, especially in Argentina. Travelling through very cold areas, a fire is one of the first things we do after setting up camp. If I'm lucky, I've managed to buy some fresh meat, tomatoes, and red peppers from one of the small village markets on the piste.

In Argentina, enjoying the deliciously rich Malbec wine is almost mandatory. A few bottles of this red nectar is most welcome at the end of a rewarding day's ride, and there's nothing better that to sit huddled around the roaring flames of your fire as you chat and re-live the best parts of the day. So, as you sit and warm yourself, why not char a couple of peppers by the fireside as you sip on your mug of wine? Cooking doesn't get any easier than this.

**WHY NOT CHAR A COUPLE OF PEPPERS BY THE FIRESIDE AS YOU SIP ON YOUR MUG OF WINE?**

Prep time: 0 minutes

Cooking time: 15 to 20 minutes (plus another 15 minutes
for "sweating"—the red pepper, not you!)

Utensils: frying pan or grill

# ROASTED RED PEPPERS

## ingredients

» *Red or orange bell peppers*

» *Olive oil*

## method

1. Place your peppers on the open grill over your fire or in a dry frying pan over your gas flame.

2. Let them roast for 15–20 minutes. Turn every few minutes, until the peppers are charred (the skin has turned black), soft and collapsing.

3. Once all the skin is charred, remove them from the heat and let sit for a couple of minutes. Once they have cooled slightly, place them into a zip-top bag and seal the bag. TIP: If you don't carry zip-top bags, any plastic bag tied tightly will do. Be careful of the hot liquid running from the pepper.

4. Leave the peppers to "sweat" for about 15 minutes. This sweating period is the secret that enables you to peel the tough skin from your peppers effortlessly.

5. Once they are cool enough to handle, you will need to de-seed and peel them.

6. Pull the stem from the top of the pepper. The stem and a clump of seeds should loosen easily.

7. Tear open the pepper, yep, with your fingers, it's a nice messy job. Remove any remaining seeds and peel off the charred skin.

8. Place the peeled and de-seeded pepper in a dish and cover with olive oil. Leave until you need it.

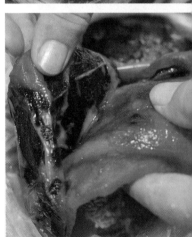

These red peppers are "oh so tasty" with a simple fried steak, or added into pasta, or as a garnish or ingredient in the Spanish Chicken recipe on page 44.

amped in the tinder-dry scrub of northern Mali we were on guard, having spent the day skirting unchecked bush fires. I needed to figure out something quick and easy to cook, but it had to be filling as it was to be our only meal of the day. I hadn't been able to pick up anything fresh. There had been no villages, no people, and, worst of all, no water. It was a hot, parched land.

We scanned the periphery as we ate, watching, waiting for any sign of fire flaring to life nearby.

Refuelled with this tasty classic, we found the energy to clear the still charred and smoking ground before setting up the tent and our camp spot. We took shifts sleeping, and neither of us managed to get much rest.

**WE SCANNED THE PERIPHERY AS WE ATE, WATCHING, WAITING FOR ANY SIGN OF FIRE FLARING TO LIFE NEARBY.**

Prep time: 10 minutes
Cooking time: 35 minutes
Utensils: 2-litre saucepan

LISA THOMAS

# QUICK CHILLI CON CARNE

## ingredients

- » *1 medium-sized onion*
- » *1 tbsp. olive oil*
- » *Salt and pepper to taste*
- » *1 can corned beef (12 oz./340g)*
- » *1 tbsp. tomato puree*
- » *½ packet (one full packet is 1.75 oz./50g) of chilli-con-carne mix or 1½ tsp. hot chilli powder (If you like a hot chilli you may need to add extra chilli powder to suit your taste.)*
- » *1 small can chopped tomatoes (15.25 oz./432g) (or fresh tomatoes, if you have them)*
- » *1 small can red kidney beans (7 oz./200g) drained (If you are unable to find red kidney beans use baked beans instead but do not add all of the sauce. Put a little of the extra sauce to one side and add later if needed. You can also use baked beans in addition to the red kidney beans for a richer flavour. The baked beans only need to heat through for 3 to 4 minutes at the end of the cooking time, any longer and they just disintegrate).*
- » *100 ml water*

## method

1. Dice the onion and then fry with the olive oil, salt, and pepper until soft.

2. Slice up the corned beef and add to the same pan. Fry them together for a few minutes.

3. Add the tomato puree and chilli mix.

4. Add the tomatoes, drained beans, and 100 ml of water. Mix and slowly bring to the boil. Once the pan is boiling, immediately turn down the heat to a simmer.

5. Simmer for about half an hour. During this simmering period, you may need to add a small amount of additional water. Stir occasionally to ensure the sauce doesn't burn on the bottom of the saucepan.

WEST AFRICA REMAINS ONE OF
THE POOREST REGIONS IN THE
WORLD

LISA THOMAS

During our time travelling through the countries of Mali, Mauritania, and Senegal, basics like fresh dairy, butter, milk, even fresh fruits and vegetables were difficult, even impossible, to find. Outside the capital cities, most "shops" are usually nothing more than a mud hut with a thatch top called a roundel, with a few shelves littered with rusty, out-of-date tins, which strangely always include sardines from Russia. Unfortunately, these taste as bad as they look. Oddly enough, the other item easily available is Happy Cow cream cheese triangles in their round box.

In the very remote areas we travel through, there are no huts, roundels, water, or even people. Our food solution in these instances is to carry a small selection of tinned foods in one of the panniers.

We are also able to carry around 50 litres of water between the two bikes, but there is a trade-off as a litre of water weighs about a kilo (2.2 pounds), which adds up to an additional 50 kilos (110 pounds). Despite carrying this amount of water we did, in fact, run out at one point whilst traversing Mali: a very dangerous situation to be in, but that's another story for another book.

So, on to the recipe …

## TIP

Serve quickly before it sets like concrete. No, I'm joking! If you have used enough oil this should not happen. I like to add a dash or two of Worcestershire sauce to my own plate once the pasta is served.

Prep time: 5 minutes
Cooking time: 12 minutes or until the pasta is al dente
Utensils: 2-litre saucepan

LISA THOMAS
······

# SARDINE SPAGHETTI

## ingredients

- » *Olive oil*
- » *Spaghetti (or whatever pasta you have) 250–300g (serves 2)*
- » *Pinch of dried mixed herbs*
- » *3 cloves garlic, finely chopped*
- » *1 large tin sardines (or 2 small tins/120g per tin) in oil or tomato sauce (if you're lucky) or substitute tins of tuna or salmon*
- » *4 triangles Happy Cow cream cheese*
- » *Salt and pepper to taste*
- » *Dash of Worcestershire sauce (aka English sauce) (optional)*

## method

1. Fill your pan 2/3 with bottled or filtered water and add a good pinch of salt.

2. Add a small glug of olive oil to the water to ensure the pasta does not stick together.

3. Add a pinch of herbs and a clove of chopped garlic.

4. Cover and bring to the boil.

5. Once the water reaches a rolling boil, add the pasta. (This is not just a few bubbles but where the whole surface is rolling.)

6. Stir once to prevent the pasta clumping together.

7. Replace the lid and bring back to the boil.

8. Once back at boiling level, remove the lid and continue to cook for the time noted on the packet or until the pasta is al-dente (with bite). This means the pasta is tender but firm to the bite. Pasta shouldn't be sloppy.

9. Drain immediately and return the cooked pasta to the saucepan.

10. Add a tablespoon of olive oil and stir in.

11. Unless the sardines are in tomato sauce, drain the tin(s) and then stir into the pasta. If your sardines are in tomato sauce simply empty the entire contents of the tin into the pan of cooked pasta and stir in well.

12. Add your 4 triangles of Happy Cow cheese (more if you like), stirring to ensure that the cheese melts into and coats the pasta.

13. Season to taste.

# 06 | MEXICAN MORSELS

With South America in our rear view mirrors, we rode north into Panama, exploring the delights of stunning Central America. Cruising through Costa Rica, Nicaragua, Honduras, and El Salvador we leant the bikes right and explored Guatemala and Belize. Across yet another border we arrived on the white shoreline of Mexico's Yucatan Peninsula. The Caribbean was already casting its spell and shellfish were on the menu.

On a hidden gem of a beach, amidst an oasis of palm trees, we set up camp and pushed our feet into the white sand. The lapping blue waters of the Caribbean was the perfect setting to cook our locally bought prawns.

Simon had scavenged hardwood, and it was already glowing red in the shallow fire pit he'd dug into the sand. With the embers spread in the pit, we threaded freshly caught prawns and pineapple chunks onto simple wooden skewers whilst enjoying the warm breeze of the Caribbean.

Heaven.

LISA THOMAS

# › how to prepare a pineapple

» *Place the pineapple on its side on a plate rather than onto a cutting board. You want to retain as much of the pineapple juice as possible for use during cooking.*

» *Cut about half an inch off the top and bottom of the pineapple.*

» *Stand the pineapple on its end and cut the skin off the sides in strips. Don't cut too thickly as you will waste too much good fruit.*

» *Continue cutting strips around the pineapple until you have cut all of the skin off.*

» *The dark brown "eyes" around the edge of the pineapple need to be removed. Carefully dig them out with the tip of your knife or the end of your potato peeler. Now you have a cylinder of pineapple flesh.*

» *Place the pineapple on its side and begin cutting into slices. Once the whole pineapple is in slices, cut the centre core from each slice. The core of the pineapple is quite hard and needs to be thrown away.*

» *Cut the cored slices roughly into cubes.*

Preparation time: 10 minutes
Cooking time: 6 minutes
Utensils: Fire pit and grill rack or BBQ plus 5 or 6 long skewers

# PINEAPPLE PRAWN PICKS

## ingredients

» *1 firm pineapple (gold to brown skin, leaves green and loose)*

» *500g/1 lb. large prawns (around 16 to 20)*

» *1 tbsp. honey*

» *Ground black pepper*

» *1 lemon or lime*

> **TIP**
>
> If you're using wooden skewers, soak them in warm water for 30 minutes beforehand so they don't burn on the fire/grill. If you have spare lemon or lime juice try soaking the skewers in juice instead of water.

## method

1. For this recipe, I alternate cubes of pineapple and prawn until each skewer is filled.

2. Make sure that the embers of the fire are spread out evenly. We carry a 10 x 8 barbeque grill that easily slides down the inside of a pannier and makes cooking on an open fire a simple process. Alternately, position two large stones in the fire so you can balance your skewers across them.

3. Wash the prawns in a bowl of fresh, clean (bottled or treated) water. Leave the shells and heads on.

4. Skewer one prawn, making sure to pass the skewer through the thickest section of the tail. Then skewer a cube of pineapple. Repeat until your skewer is full and make sure that the pineapple pieces and prawns are pushed together firmly.

5. Pour the pineapple juice (retained from when you were chopping) into a mug and add a tablespoon of honey and a little ground black pepper. Mix well and use a little to baste the prawn and pineapple before placing over the fire.

6. Place your skewers over the hot embers and cook for two or three minutes per side, continually basting with the sauce. They're cooked when they turn a charred pink colour.

7. Pour any remaining sauce over the prawns.

8. Serve with rice or just eat on their own.

# 07 | THE SPICE OF LIFE
# INDIA

LISA THOMAS

O ur travels through India were intoxicating, our senses bombarded with the hustle and bustle of life and the fragrance of mixed spices and exotic ingredients that emanate from every kitchen.

**FOOD, SPICE, AND SUBTLE FLAVOURS ARE BLENDED AND PREPARED IN INDIA UNLIKE ANYWHERE ELSE IN THE WORLD.**

Learning how to cook a "real" curry with local families was delicious and exciting.

Luckily both Simon and I love a goody curry; not so lucky in that I like a good hot one and Simon prefers the milder version. Who wins? Simon, of course. Although, just to keep him on his toes, I surprise him with a hot one now and again and don't tell him!

You can make this quick and easy curry as mild or as spicy as you like. I use the traditional spices and love the process of preparing them even after a long day of riding. I find prepping and cooking food enables me to decompress and absorb the day's adventures.

Don't worry if you don't have all the separate spices, plain curry powder also produces surprisingly tasty results.

# LISA'S CIKANA KARI (CHICKEN CURRY)

## ingredients

» 1½ cups/360 ml chicken stock

» ½ tsp. mustard seeds

» ½ tsp. coriander/cilantro seeds

» ½ tsp. cumin seeds

» 500g/1lb chicken meat (Any parts you can get that look half decent. Chop into chucks with or without the bone. You can use beef instead of chicken. If using beef, use a beef stock cube.)

» 2 tbsp. oil

» One medium onion, finely sliced

» One medium apple peeled, cored, and chopped into small chunks

» 2 heaped tsps. curry powder (This does depend upon the strength of the powder and how hot you like your curries.)

» A handful of sultanas, chopped (Alternately, use chopped dried apricots or dates.)

» 2 tbsp. chutney (Mango chutney is best but any sweet chutney or orange marmalade or apricot jam are good substitutes.)

» ¼ tsp. garam masala powder (Garam masala is a blend of ground spices common to north India.)

» 2 tbsp. tomato ketchup or 1 tbsp. tomato puree (The ketchup is only needed to deepen the colour of the sauce, which makes it look richer and more appetizing. The ketchup doesn't have a substantial impact on the flavour.)

# method

1. If you serve rice with this dish, cook it beforehand so it can sit "steaming" whilst you are cooking the curry. (See rice recipe on page 77.)

2. Prepare the stock. Place stock cube in a separate bowl and add 360 ml (1½ cups) of boiling water. Stir until the stock cube dissolves.

3. Place the seeds in a small cup and grind with the back of a spoon. Or if you carry one, use a small pestle and mortar—I wish I had one of these.

4. Chop the chicken into pieces around the size that will sit in a tablespoon as this size won't take too long to cook.

5. Heat 2 tbsp. of oil in your pan. Add the lightly-crushed coriander, cumin, and mustard seeds.

6. Swirl the seeds around in the hot oil as this will flavour the oil and prevent them from burning. Cook for 2 minutes.

7. Add the sliced onions and chopped apple to the spices and oil in the pan and fry and stir gently for a few seconds to ensure all pieces are coated in the spices and oil.

8. Add the curry powder stir until the onion and apple are completely coated in the powder.

9. Add the chunks of chicken. Fry the chunks for 3 to 4 minutes on both sides. Make sure they are well coated with the curry powder. (You may need to add 2 to 3 tablespoons of stock at this point to prevent this mixture from drying out too much and scorching the bottom of the pan.)

10. Add just enough stock to cover the mixture. Stir well and bring to a simmer.

11. Simmer uncovered for 15 minutes. Stir gently a couple of times during cooking.

12. After the 15 minutes cooking time, taste the curry in order to check its spiciness. If more curry powder is required, this is the time to add it in. It's best to sprinkle the additional powder on the top and gently stir in.

13. Add the final items: sultanas, chutney, garam masala, and the tomato sauce. Stir in well.

14. Cook uncovered for a further 15 minutes. It's during this cooking time that the sauce should begin to thicken. The chutney helps with the thickening process. If the sauce hasn't thickened as much as you would like, mix 2 tbsp. of water with 1 teaspoon of corn flour or cornstarch in a cup. Mix it until it's smooth and then add slowly to the curry, gently stirring in so it doesn't make lumps. Let the sauce cook for a further 2 minutes, and it should thicken nicely.

15. Serve with boiled rice.

Prep time:  5 minutes
Cooking time: 45 minutes
Utensils: 2-litre saucepan

# 08 | BUSH TUCKER IN AUSTRALIA

After travelling for years through Muslim countries, Simon and I had built up a healthy craving for some really juicy pork. We'd even started fantasizing about bacon sandwiches. We both knew that this was one craving that was only going to be satisfied when we reached our 6th Continent: Australia.

Simon and I had planned for years to attempt one of Australia's toughest routes, the aptly named World's Longest Shortcut. This route runs diagonally from Australia's northeast coastline all the way across to Perth on its far southwest shores. It consists of 2,500 kms of dirt, sand tracks, and sun-bleached desert.

At the route's halfway point I was beaten and bruised. My cravings had pushed a forgotten recipe to the front of my brain, and I was already salivating. Thankfully it is quick to prepare, sweet, delicious, and now needed only to be cooked.

In a small outback town I found pork and a few other key ingredients to combine with the supplies I carry on my bike. At the end of one long day's ride, we set up camp and treated ourselves to this tasty pork recipe and stared spellbound at the star-studded night sky, relishing the solitude of Australia's Outback.

SIMON AND I HAD PLANNED FOR YEARS TO ATTEMPT ONE OF AUSTRALIA'S TOUGHEST ROUTES, THE APTLY NAMED WORLD'S LONGEST SHORTCUT—2,500 KMS OF DIRT, SAND TRACKS, AND SUN-BLEACHED DESERT.

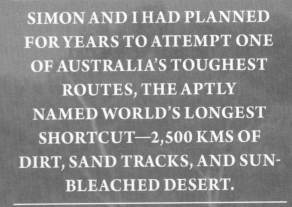

# ORANGE PORK

 **ingredients**

- » 2 medium-sized oranges, juiced (Approx. 120 ml/1/2 cup.)
- » 2 tablespoons orange marmalade (Or if you haven't been lucky enough to find marmalade use 2 tablespoons of honey and add the orange flesh from one of the oranges chopped into pieces along with 8 chopped dates.)
- » 1 tbsp. whole-grain mustard
- » 1 tbsp. olive oil
- » 500g/1 lb. pork chunks (at least 1-inch thick)
- » ¼ tsp. salt
- » ¼ tsp. freshly ground black pepper
- » 2 fresh rosemary sprigs or ½ tsp. dried rosemary
- » 1 medium onion, cut into 1/2-inch wedges . (A red onion is best.)
- » 2 carrots, sliced
- » 1 medium potato, cubed (The smaller the cube, the faster the potato will cook. Alternately, omit the potatoes and serve with rice cooked separately instead.)
- » 2 tablespoons fresh lime juice (or 1 tbsp. bottled concentrated lime juice)

## method

1. Combine the juice, marmalade, or honey mix along with the mustard in a saucepan over medium-high heat. Bring to a boil, reduce the heat, and simmer until syrupy. Keep this simmering until you need it.

2. Add oil into a separate pan over a medium-high heat.

3. Season the pork with salt and pepper. Add the pork to your pan and cook for five minutes, stirring occasionally until the meat is browned.

4. Add the rosemary, onion, carrots, and cubed potatoes to pan. Cook for a further five minutes.

5. Pour the juice mixture over the pork. Stir in well, making sure the pork and all the vegetables are coated with the sauce.

6. Continue to cook on a low flame until the potatoes are tender. Stir occasionally to stop it from catching on the bottom of the pan. You may need to add a couple more tablespoons of water if the potatoes absorb too much of the liquid.

7. Add the lime juice once the potatoes are cooked. Then cook a further 2 minutes. The liquid should be syrupy.

Prep time: 5 minutes
Cooking time: 35 minutes
Utensils: 2-litre saucepan and a frying pan

# 09 | RICE KARMA NEPAL

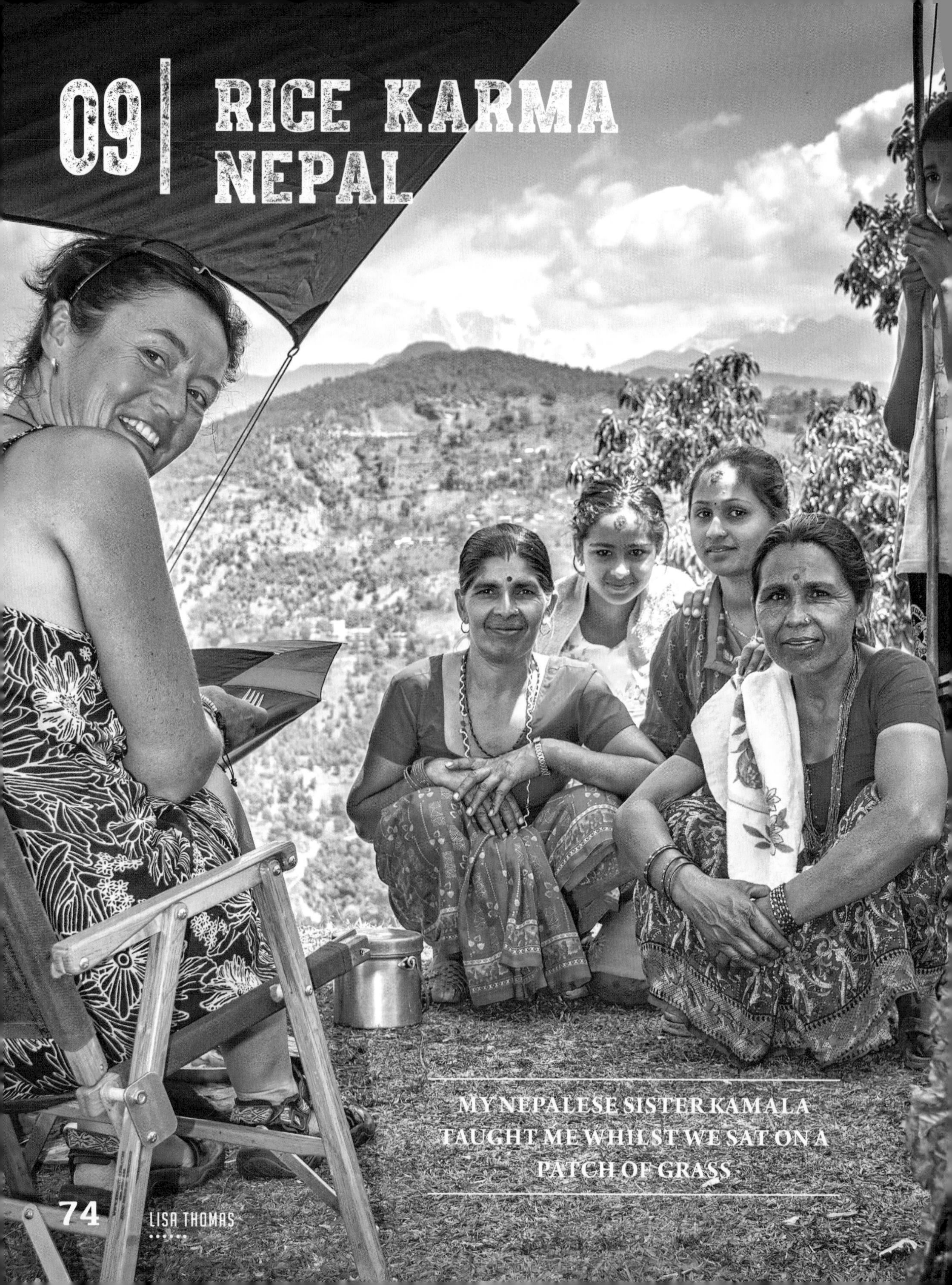

MY NEPALESE SISTER KAMALA
TAUGHT ME WHILST WE SAT ON A
PATCH OF GRASS

LISA THOMAS

**Y**eah—I know this sounds silly. Surely any dumbo can cook rice. Well . . . I'm not so sure.

I used to have a problem with my rice being overcooked. I just couldn't seem to get the quantities right and nothing I tried worked. My Nepalese sister Kamala taught me this recipe whilst we sat on a patch of grass in front of the majestic Annapurna Himalayas with the sacred mountain Machhapuchhre looking down upon us.

Rice is one item that we have found available around the world. However, it's often found in open bags on the ground, having been dried on the road beforehand. You will need to rinse it thoroughly (if you have the water to spare) and check through the grains for road grit. Otherwise you can easily break a tooth; a hard lesson learnt from experience.

Prep time: 2 minutes
Cooking time: 15 minutes including steaming time
Utensils: 2-litre saucepan

# PERFECTLY COOKED RICE

## ingredients

» *Rice (a generous handful per person)*

» *Water*

» *Salt*

## variations

» *Add turmeric.*

» *Add cardamom seeds.*

» *Add herbs and garlic into the water during cooking.*

» *Place a stock cube in the water instead of salt.*

## method

1. Place your rice in a saucepan. If it's the rice from the large open bags (read the story above), then check through the rice and rinse well.

2. Cover with cold water but only cover so that the water is one "knuckle-depth" over the rice. Look at your knuckles; it's just one segment of your finger, that's the correct amount of water that should be above your rice regardless as to the size of the pan or the amount of rice.

3. Add a pinch of salt into the water.

4. Cover with the lid and bring to the boil.

5. Boil for 2 to 3 minutes then take off the heat and put to one side leaving the lid on.

6. After 10 minutes lift the lid and have a look at the rice. If all the water is absorbed then give it a quick stir——this fluffs up the rice nicely. If there is still a bit more water that needs to be absorbed then put the lid back on and leave for another few minutes.

7. To check if the rice is cooked properly test it by tasting a few grains. If it requires a few more minutes of cooking add a tablespoon or two of water, give the pan a shake. Place the lid back on and return to the heat for 2 minutes.

8. After the additional 2 minutes remove from the heat and leave covered until your main dish is ready. Stir the rice to fluff it up and serve.

# 10 | MANAGING IN MONGOLIA

LISA THOMAS

If you're in search of raw, untamed adventure and love the idea of riding across wide, windswept plains or seas of dunes, then Mongolia is hard to beat. Steeped in ancient history and tradition many Mongols still practice the same nomadic traditions as the generations before them. The legendary Mongol ruler, the great Genghis Khan, once ruled two-thirds of the world from this landlocked country.

In what is one of the least inhabited countries on the planet, hundreds of miles can separate nomadic villages, and food can be scarce. Local provisions, when you are out on the Steppe or in the Gobi desert, are few and far between. When you do find a small village, the foodstuffs available may often be limited to stale biscuits, out-of-date Mars bars or Snickers and crisps (chips). In another small hut, you may find a few carrots, potatoes, and onions that have all seen better days and, if you are extremely lucky, some processed sausage meat. There is absolutely nothing green apart from the few strands of grass you rode in on.

It was on one of our many long, cold, and dusty days riding that I decided to throw together one of my "fail-safe" recipes. It's also very quick to cook and warms you right through. The special addition at the end of this recipe is a real treat on a cold, barren Mongolian night.

LISA THOMAS

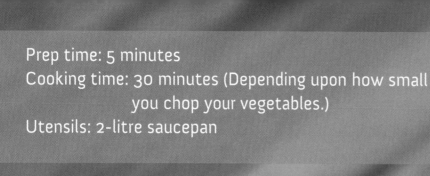

Prep time: 5 minutes
Cooking time: 30 minutes (Depending upon how small
you chop your vegetables.)
Utensils: 2-litre saucepan

## TIP

Add a little salt and pepper to taste but remember that the packet soup will already have a high salt content and you may have used less water than is required to just make a soup. So, make sure you taste first before adding. You can use any packet soup but clear chicken noodle and clear vegetable work best.

# MAKE-DO
# MONGOLIAN STEW

## ingredients

» 1 processed sausage, or 1 small tin of Spam, cut into small bite-sized pieces (You might also use bacon, diced beef or lamb, but these meats require a longer cooking time.)

» Dash of oil (I like to use olive oil when I can as it adds more flavour.)

» 1 medium onion, chopped medium fine

» 1 large potato or 3 to 4 small, cut into bite-sized pieces (Smaller pieces will cook faster.)

» 1 carrot, cut into bite-sized pieces

» Pinch of dry mixed herbs

» Pinch of chilli powder or dash of tabasco sauce

» Packet of chicken noodle soup or vegetable soup (the size that makes 1 litre and serves 4)

» 1 small can (220g/8 oz.) mixed veg or corn

» Shredded Parmesan cheese is preferable but in reality any cheese will do (optional)

» Salt and pepper to taste

## method

1. Fry the sausage pieces (or Spam) in a little oil until browned. Remove them from the pan and leave to the side ready for last minute addition when everything else is cooked. A lightly browned sausage or Spam is more appealing to eat.

2. In the remaining oil, brown the onions.

3. Add the potato and carrots into the pan with a pinch of mixed herbs and stir.

4. Add a pinch of chilli powder or dash of Tabasco for a little zing.

5. Take the pan off the heat for a few moments whilst you add the packet of soup, stirring well so that the powder covers the vegetables evenly.

6. Then (still off the heat) add enough water to just cover the vegetables and stir well.

7. Place the pan back on the heat, keep stirring every few seconds so that it doesn't go lumpy.

8. Bring to a simmer. This is where the bubbles are forming and gently rising to the surface rather than the full rolling boil.

9. Stir occasionally to prevent sticking or burning.

10. Add more water a little at a time during cooking to ensure it doesn't get gloopy. Remember you want this to be more stewy than soupy.

11. Once you are happy that the vegeables are cooked to your liking, add the already-cooked sausage/Spam and can of veg/corn.

12. Heat through for another 2 minutes before serving.

13. Sprinkle with parmesan cheese, if using, and serve with bread. If no bread, then have a shot of that vodka you've been able to carry as that makes up for everything.

# 11 | STEWING IN PAKISTAN

It was late December when we arrived in Islamabad, Pakistan. We camped in a military protected park in the centre of the city whilst waiting for our Indian visas to be processed. Temperatures didn't get above freezing during the day and a warming stew sounded like just the thing.

Walking through the open markets in Islamabad, I asked for memna (lamb) or bakri (goat) to include in my stew. Lamb is one of the favourite meats in Pakistan.

During cooking, a few of the guards, wrapped in their thin blankets, would come and join us for a cup of hot tea before slowly walking off into the dark to do their perimeter check. These guys lived very basically in meagre facilities. Our camping kit amazed them just as their tents and chapatti ovens amazed us. Simon spent many a cold morning having coffee with the men whilst being allowed to take photos. This was a real privilege and made up for the frustrating period of waiting for bureaucracy.

This recipe is a combination of lamb, lentils, and tomatoes in a curry-based stew. To be truthful, lamb is difficult to find in many countries and goat meat is the only real alternative.

This dish does take a little while to cook, as you don't want the meat to be tough. However, if you start it early enough, it can just continue to simmer as you busy yourself with downloading all the photos you took that day or write your journal. You just need to occasionally stir the stew to make sure it's not burning (catching on the bottom) and add a small amount of water if it's drying out too much. If you want the sauce to be a little spicier, add a little more curry powder during cooking. Other than that, leave it alone and get your work done.

Prep time: 6 minutes
Cooking time: 1 hour 20 minutes
Utensils: 2-litre saucepan

# LAMTIL STEW

## ingredients

- » 500g/1 lb. pound boneless lamb or goat cut into 1-inch pieces
- » Salt and pepper
- » 1 tbsp. olive oil
- » 1 large chopped onion
- » 2 garlic cloves, minced
- » 1 tsp. minced peeled (fresh) ginger or ½ tsp. powdered ginger
- » 1 tbsp. curry powder (Depending upon the strength of the powder. So it may be best to use a little less and then add extra during cooking for more heat.)
- » 480 ml water, approx. 2 cups
- » 3 carrots, peeled, thickly sliced
- » 240g/1 cup dried green or brown lentils
- » 360g/1½ cups canned diced tomatoes in juice or 3 medium fresh tomatoes, chopped
- » One small tin peas

## method

1. Sprinkle lamb with salt and pepper to season.

2. Heat oil in your largest saucepan over medium to high heat.

3. Add the lamb to the saucepan and sauté until brown, about 5 minutes.

4. Add onion, garlic, and ginger. Sauté for an additional 5 minutes.

5. Add curry powder; stir for 30 seconds.

6. Add 2 cups (480 ml) water and the carrots, lentils, and tomatoes. Stir and bring to a boil.

7. Reduce heat, cover and simmer until lamb and lentils are tender, stirring occasionally, about 1 hour.

8. Add peas to pot and simmer until heated through, about 5 minutes.

**Serve in bowls.**

# 12

# CRUISING IN BAJA

LISA THOMAS

Creamy Mushroom Pork is another recipe I've brought from home. After a hard day in the office and an hour's horrible commute back home, this dish was a saviour. It is quick and easy to prepare and the ideal comfort food on long, dark nights. You're going to love it.

These days I cook it in a saucepan on top of my MSR stove whilst sitting in my Kermit chair beside my motorcycle. Perfect!

Prep time: 3 minutes
Cooking time: 25 to 30 minutes
Utensils: 2-litre saucepan

LISA THOMAS

# CREAMY MUSHROOM PORK

## ingredients

- » *1 tbsp. olive oil*
- » *I small onion, chopped*
- » *2 garlic cloves, chopped*
- » *500g/1 lb. boneless pork, or chicken, cut into 1" cubes.*
- » *One 420g/10¾ oz. can condensed cream of mushroom soup (I prefer to use Campbell's soup if I can find it.)*
- » *One 200g/7.7 oz. tin of corn or mixed vegetables (drained)*
- » *2 tbsp. milk (Or use dried milk powder mixed up with water.)*
- » *Dash of soy sauce*

## variations

- » *Use 2 thick pork chops.*
- » *Add some finely chopped fresh mushrooms or a small can of (drained) mushrooms.*
- » *Fry some chopped zucchini along with the onion and garlic.*

## method

1. Heat the oil in your frying pan over a medium heat.
2. Add the chopped onion and garlic and brown.
3. Add the pork and cook for 10 minutes, stirring so the pieces are all well browned.
4. Stir in the can of condensed soup. Mix well and bring to a boil. Do not add any additional water or milk.
5. Reduce the heat to a simmer.
6. Cover with a lid and cook for a further 10 minutes.
7. Add the drained can of mixed vegetables or corn and cook for another 5 minutes.
8. Stir occasionally to prevent the sauce from catching on the bottom of the saucepan. You may need to add a tablespoon or two of milk if the sauce is becoming too thick, but the sauce shouldn't be thin like a soup.
9. Serve with boiled rice. Add a dash of soy sauce to your plate once served.

The Spanish tortilla became a favourite dish of ours during our time camping on the outskirts of a Nepalese village cradled in a valley below the mighty Annapurna Mountain Range. All of the ingredients were easy to obtain from the ramshackle wooden huts that precariously balanced on their wooden stilts, seemingly hovering above the paddy fields.

In the evenings we enjoyed the tortilla with a cheap Nepali beer called "Everest" whilst watching the fields being prepared in readiness for the monsoon season. The rice paddies extended as a beautiful green patchwork carved up into the hillsides above us for as far as the eye could see. It was a very peaceful and restful period.

## TIP

These Spanish tortillas are great eaten at room temperature with a good cold beer. If it's a cold/cool climate you can carry some pieces with you on the road in readiness for a quick roadside snack. Eat on its own or with a tin of tuna and sliced tomato.

Prep time: 5 minutes
Cooking time: 25 minutes
Utensils: 2-litre saucepan and frying pan

# SPANISH TORTILLA

## ingredients

» *1 large potato, thinly sliced*
» *1 large onion, thinly sliced*
» *2 cloves garlic, finely chopped*
» *Olive oil*
» *3 medium-sized eggs, beaten until frothy*
» *Salt and pepper*

I cheat when I cook my tortilla. The traditional way is to gently fry the onion and potato, constantly turning so neither gets browned nor burnt. This takes a lot of attention. So, for speed, I use the following method.

## method

1. Boil the potato slices until almost cooked. You don't want to overcook these otherwise they will just fall apart when you come to place them in your frying pan.

2. Drain and place to one side.

3. Separately fry the onions and garlic in your frying pan ensuring they don't burn.

4. Once cooked remove from the pan and place to one side on a separate plate.

5. Off the heat place a little oil in the frying pan. Make sure the whole surface of the frying pan is covered with a film of oil.

6. Place the potato and onion/garlic in alternate layers in your frying pan starting with the onion first and finishing with a layer of onion.

7. Return the frying pan to the heat.

8. The potato layers will begin to cook once the oil has heated.

9. Cook for 2 minutes. Do not stir.

10. Pour the beaten egg mixture over the now cooking layers.

11. Move the pan gently side to side to ensure all of the potato and onion layers are covered with the egg mixture.

12. When the underside is cooked remove from the heat and place a plate over the top of the frying pan, like a lid. Using a cloth to hold the plate in place, in one swift movement flip the pan and plate over, leaving the partially cooked ingredients now on the plate.

13. Now, here's the trick: you are going to slide the tortilla from the plate back into the frying pan to cook the other side.

14. Once both sides are browned, remove from the pan and place on a separate plate.

## variation

» *Add some finely chopped chilli and sliced zucchini.*

# 14 | NEW ZEALAND THE SOUTH ISLAND

I have adapted this a lot since leaving home. My version is fast and cheap and mostly uses tins and other items that you will have in your small selection of provisions.

I know you will ask "Ah, but what about the eggs that I see in the list of ingredients. You have to have bought those on the day?" Nope. I manage to carry eggs with me in one of my water bags on top of my pannier. They have never cracked or broken, but I do make sure that I tie them in a plastic bag just in case. No one wants a gooey, sticky egg mess to clean out of a motorcycle bag.

IT MAKES IT A GREAT MEAL FOR WHEN YOU HAVE NOT BEEN ABLE TO BUY ANY FRESH ITEMS AND ARE IN THE MIDDLE OF NOWHERE.

# SIMPLE STIR-FRIED RICE

## ingredients

- » *2 tbsp. olive oil*
- » *1 medium onion (red or brown), finely chopped*
- » *1 chilli, deseeded and chopped (optional)*
- » *Chopped garlic (optional)*
- » *1 small tin Spam (198g/7 oz.), chopped into bite-sized pieces (Or a tin of tuna, drained, added right at the end of cooking. It's possible to use any kind of meat but cook it fully beforehand and then add to the rice mixture.)*
- » *1 cereal bowl cooked rice (See recipe on page 77.)*
- » *1 small tin corn, drained (225g/8 oz.)*
- » *1 small tin mushrooms, drained (225g/8 oz.)*
- » *1 small tin mixed vegetables, drained (225g/8 oz.) (Or use a selection of fresh vegetables if you can. If using fresh, quickly stir-fry them before adding them into the rice.)*
- » *2 eggs*
- » *Salt and pepper*
- » *Soy sauce*

## method

1. In your frying pan or saucepan (whichever is the larger) heat up a tbsp. of oil then add the chopped onion. Fry until it begins to get see-through.

2. Add the chopped chilli and garlic (if using) and stir-fry for a further 30 seconds.

3. Add the chopped Spam and stir-fry until it takes on some colour. Spam always looks better in my opinion when it doesn't look pale.

4. Add the cooked rice and stir until every grain of rice has a coating of oil. Keep it moving (you don't want your rice to burn) so that the rice heats through.

5. Add some ground black pepper.

6. Once the rice has heated through and is nicely coated with the olive oil, empty in your drained selection of tinned vegetables or fresh stir-fried vegetables.

7. Stir well. Heat through thoroughly and stir a couple of times every minute.

8. Whilst this final mixed rice mixture is heating through, beat two eggs in a cup with a little salt and pepper.

9. Pour the beaten eggs over the cooking mixed rice and vegetables. Let the eggs start to cook a little before stirring into the rice and vegetables.

10. Keep stirring until the egg has coated the grains of rice and is cooked.

11. Serve with a dash of soy sauce.

Prep time: 3 minutes
Cooking time: 15 minutes
Utensils: frying pan

## TIP

I always cook my rice and allow it to sit awhile before I need it. It sits as I prep the tent for the night, put our riding kit away in the tent, and generally tidy up.

Make sure that the rice is covered and insects are not able to crawl into your meal, otherwise, you will have an extra meat ration!

# 15 | INDIA
# THE GREAT THAR DESERT

**T**hai Green Vegetable Curry may sound a bit exotic for this type of cookbook, however, if you are carrying green curry paste (available in single packets these days) and a small carton of long life cream, all you really need are a variety of vegetables. I have found that the long life cartons of cream last for a couple of months, regardless of temperature, with no problems.

The recipe on the next page offers a few variations and ideas for substitutions. I've cooked this in many different countries, but the one that sticks in my mind is the time I cooked it in the Great Thar Desert in the far west of India. For the sake of our sanity, we needed a few nights of solitude, almost impossible in what is the second most populated country in the world. Skirting the Great Thar Desert, we detoured and simply rode into the dunes. When the bikes became stuck in the deep sand, we made camp. We were only 33 miles away from the border with Pakistan.

Around 20 minutes before making camp we rode past a small village and managed to pick up all of the vegetables required in this recipe. These, along with items from my provisions, made an excellent vegetable green curry.

We had just finished our day and were enjoying the sunset when over the dunes walked a solitary figure, silhouetted by the setting sun. A local shepherd had seen our campfire and stopped to say hello. With our new friend walking into the night we sat in our Kermit chairs eating our curry in front of a roaring fire and watched the stars erupt in a pitch-black sky. Bliss.

LISA THOMAS

WE SAT IN OUR CHAIRS
EATING OUR CURRY AND
WATCHED THE STARS
ERUPT IN A PITCH-BLACK
SKY. BLISS.

Prep time: 3 minutes
Cooking time: 25 to 30 minutes
Utensils: 2-litre saucepan

# THAI GREEN VEGETABLE CURRY

## ingredients

- » 1 tbsp. olive oil
- » 2 tsp. ready-made green curry paste
- » 1 (250ml) carton long life cream or coconut cream
- » 1 medium eggplant chopped into chunks (Thai eggplant "apple eggplant" is best. Or, instead of eggplant, use tofu, but only add the tofu into the sauce at point 9, the final stage of cooking. If you want to change this to a non-vegetarian dish, add a good handful of boneless chicken breast per person, diagonally sliced, 1/2-inch thick.)
- » 1 medium or 2 small zucchini, chopped into chunks
- » 1 small handful green beans, sliced diagonally into 1-inch-long pieces
- » 1 small red pepper, sliced into thin strips
- » 3 small firm tomatoes, chopped into chunks
- » 1 small green chilli, sliced finely (optional)
- » Bok choy (optional)
- » Juice and zest of 1 small lime
- » 1 tsp. sugar

## method

1. Heat the oil in a saucepan over a medium-high heat. Add the onion and cook, stirring occasionally, until softened, 3 to 4 minutes.

2. Add the green curry paste into your pan and stir well over a low heat for one minute, ensuring the paste doesn't burn.

3. Add in the cream.

4. Stir until the paste and cream are completely mixed into a creamy green sauce.

5. If you're cooking the non-vegetarian version and using chicken, now is the time to add your slices of chicken.

6. Add in the zucchini and green beans. Mix well.

7. Add in the eggplant. Gently mix in ensuring all the vegetables are coated with the sauce.

8. Add 1 cup of water. Reduce heat and simmer, partially covered, until the eggplant is tender or your chicken is completely cooked, around 12 to 15 minutes. The eggplant needs to be cooked until it is soft and creamy.

9. Add the red pepper, tomatoes, tofu, chilli, and bok choy (if using these three items), lime zest, juice and sugar.

10. Stir well and cook for a further 10 minutes.

# 16 | SUCCULENT SLICES IN ARGENTINA

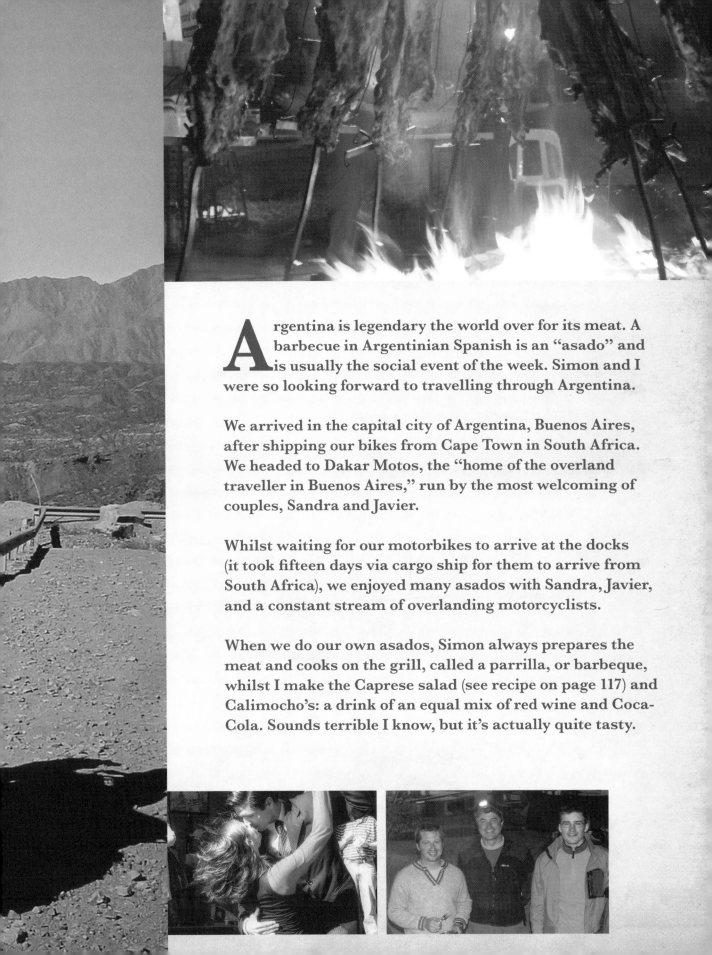

Argentina is legendary the world over for its meat. A barbecue in Argentinian Spanish is an "asado" and is usually the social event of the week. Simon and I were so looking forward to travelling through Argentina.

We arrived in the capital city of Argentina, Buenos Aires, after shipping our bikes from Cape Town in South Africa. We headed to Dakar Motos, the "home of the overland traveller in Buenos Aires," run by the most welcoming of couples, Sandra and Javier.

Whilst waiting for our motorbikes to arrive at the docks (it took fifteen days via cargo ship for them to arrive from South Africa), we enjoyed many asados with Sandra, Javier, and a constant stream of overlanding motorcyclists.

When we do our own asados, Simon always prepares the meat and cooks on the grill, called a parrilla, or barbeque, whilst I make the Caprese salad (see recipe on page 117) and Calimocho's: a drink of an equal mix of red wine and Coca-Cola. Sounds terrible I know, but it's actually quite tasty.

# MEAT-FEST ASADO

## ingredients

» *Coarse sea salt*

» *Steak, one per person*

» *Approx. 500g/1 lb. per person costillas (ribs) or asado de tira (short-ribs)*

» *Chorizo (a pork and smoked paprika sausage)*

» *Morcillas (aka blood sausage)*

» *Chimichurri sauce (herb-and-vinegar sauce) (I cheat and buy the shop-made chimichurri available almost everywhere in Argentina.)*

## method

1. The meat of an Argentinian asado is not smothered in sweet, smoky barbecue sauce. It is simply salted with coarse sea salt and placed on the grill.

2. Prepare your grill using either wood or charcoal, heating the coals until they are white and hot.

3. Salt both sides of your steak and ribs liberally. Massage the salt into the meat slightly. DO NOT use fine salt; only coarse salt will do. Fine salt will just dry the meat out.

4. Place the ribs on the grill.

5. After about 10–15 minutes, turn the ribs over and let them grill another 15 minutes or so until the meat is brown and juicy.

6. At this point, place the chorizo and morcilla onto the grill. Keep turning so they cook evenly and don't burn.

7. Once cooked, remove the ribs and sausages from the grill and let them sit to one side as you are cooking your steak.

8. Place your steak on the grill and cook to your liking.

9. Serve the meat and sausages with chimichurri sauce, an Argentinian Malbec (red wine) or calimocho's and Caprese salad. (See recipe on page 117.)

Prep time: 3 minutes

Cooking time: However you like your steak plus 30+ minutes for the other meats.

Utensils: a parrilla (BBQ) or open fire

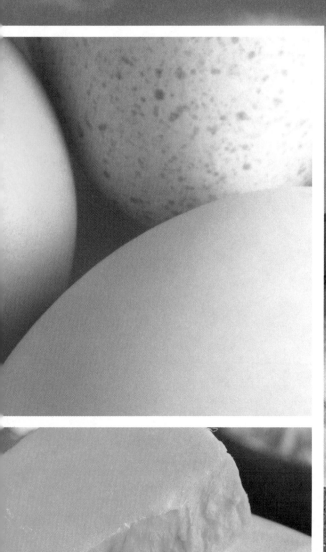

Prep time: 3 minutes
Cooking time: 10 minutes
Utensils: frying pan

YOU'RE TIRED, COLD, AND IT'S STILL RAINING BUT YOU NEED TO EAT. WHAT TO DO FOR THAT QUICK MEAL? AN OMELETTE, OF COURSE!

Prep time: 3 minutes
Cooking time: 25 to 30 minutes
Utensils: 2-litre saucepan

# OMELETTE
## (& VARIED FILLINGS)

An omelette can be stuffed with an endless variety of savory foods. Here are our "on the road" favourite fillings.

## ingredients

» *2 eggs per person*

» *Salt and pepper (pinch)*

» *Oil*

## fillings

*All of these mixtures need to be spooned into half of the almost-cooked omelette before folding the other half of the omelette over the mixture, enclosing the filling.*

» *Half a tin tuna (70g) per omelette plus two Happy Cow cream cheese triangles. Mash the tuna and cheese together. Add ground pepper.*

» *Mushrooms and onion. Cook beforehand and place to one side until needed.*

» *A real treat: bacon and blue cheese. Yeah, I know that blue cheese is not a good idea to carry on a motorbike, but this is a great breakfast/snack/meal when spending a night in a hostel with a fridge and cook area. Cook the bacon beforehand and then crumble the blue cheese on top before folding the omelette.*

» *Spinach. Wash well, remove stems and shred the leaves. Place on one half of the omelette.*

» *Optional: Add some crumbled blue cheese before folding.*

» *Ham, chorizo or Spam, spring onions, and a small chilli (optional) chopped and fried beforehand and placed to one side until the omelette is almost cooked.*

## method

1. Place the eggs, salt and pepper in a bowl.

2. Use a fork to whisk the eggs until they are thoroughly mixed.

3. Heat ½ tablespoon of oil in your frying pan until it's sizzling. The oil and pan have to be hot enough to cook the omelette quickly underneath whilst the top remains soft.

4. Pour the whisked eggs into the pan and tilt so that the mixture covers the base.

5. As the egg mixture begins to set use your spatula to pull the outer edge of the setting omelette into the middle, tilting the pan again so that uncooked egg runs underneath and out to the sides.

6. Cook for 1 to 2 minutes or until golden and just set underneath.

7. The top needs to be slightly runny as this continues to cook when you fold the omelette or fill with your chosen filling.

The omelette is now ready to slide onto your plate. Or you can eat it straight from the frying pan.

Travelling through Italy on two motorbikes we made the most of the Italian olive oils, mozzarella, and fresh bread. When it was hot, this made a great side to a main course or accompanied with mixed salad and a tasty bottle of good Italian wine.

Salad, mozzarella, good fresh bread, and a bottle of Italian wine are not easily found (understatement) in many parts of the world. The other problem is that carrying fresh cheese and green salads on a motorbike for any distance in the heat will lead to a gooey mess and fermenting green sludge.

Remember, lettuce bruises easily, so shoving it into a bag or strapping it down with a bungee will ruin it in seconds.

There have been times when we craved fresh, healthy vegetables. Luckily, tomatoes are available in most countries. After hearing how tomatoes are fertilized in many parts of the world, I always make sure to wash them well! Unfortunately, locating a good quality cheese is more of an issue.

# CAPRESE SALAD
## (TOMATO AND MOZZARELLA)

## ingredients

» *5 ripe tomatoes (any type, but I like plum tomatoes best) cut into 1/4-inch-thick slices*

» *500g/1 lb. fresh mozzarella, cut into 1/4-inch-thick slices (I like to use buffalo mozzarella—little white mozzarella balls—but when I have been unable to locate anything like this I use any type of cheese apart from feta. Feta crumbles too easily. As a 'desperate' alternative I substitute with Happy Cow cheese triangles cut into small chunks.)*

» *20 to 30 leaves, or about 1 bunch, of fresh basil (Dried basil is a very poor substitute here but if you have to use it, measure out only 2 tsp.)*

» *Olive oil for drizzling*

» *Salt and pepper*

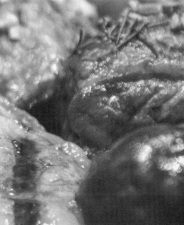

## method

1. Layer alternating slices of tomatoes and mozzarella, adding a basil leaf (or pinch of dried basil) between each, on your plate.

2. Drizzle the salad with olive oil (extra-virgin, if you have it).

3. Season with salt and pepper.

LISA THOMAS

This is a quick and warming soup and always makes me think of home and family as my mother used to make it as a winter lunchtime special. I just grab whatever vegetables are around and use this recipe as a basic rule of thumb to follow. The bacon really does make it, though.

Prep time: 3 minutes
Cooking time: 10 minutes
Utensils: 2-litre saucepan

# ITALIAN SOUP

## variations

» *Mushrooms (canned or fresh)*

» *Small chopped potatoes*

» *Small can of mixed vegetables*

» *Chopped celery*

» *After serving add some drops of Tabasco sauce to add a bit of zing*

» *Omit the bacon and just use a little more ham*

## ingredients

» *1 tbsp. olive oil*

» *5 slices streaky bacon*

» *1 onion, chopped*

» *1 garlic clove, finely chopped*

» *1 carrot, chopped*

» *1 bunch of spring onions, chopped (or substitute with a small onion, chopped)*

» *1 litre/4 cups chicken or vegetable stock*

» *Handful of pasta shells (If you don't have any pasta shells—and I normally don't—I break up my spaghetti into small bite-sized pieces. If you don't have any pasta, use a small handful of rice.)*

» *5 slices (sandwich-sized) cooked ham, cut into narrow ½-inch strips*

» *1 small (220g/8 oz.) can corn, drained*

» *Salt and pepper*

» *Grated Parmesan cheese*

## method

1. Heat the oil in a pan and fry the bacon gently for 2 minutes.

2. Add the onion, garlic, carrots, and fry for 5 minutes.

3. Add the stock and bring to the boil, cover and cook over a medium flame for 10 minutes.

4. Add the pasta and cook until pasta is al dente; around 10 minutes or less depending upon the type of pasta used.

5. Add the ham and corn, stir and cook for 2 minutes.

6. Salt and pepper to taste. If you are lucky enough to be carrying with you a packet or small tin of Parmesan cheese, sprinkle this on the top.

# 20 | MOROCCAN MAIN COURSE

In Morocco, couscous is served with a dish called a tagine. This dish is a spicy or mild stew made of carrots, potatoes, and turnips with usually lamb, mutton, or goat meat. I first tasted couscous when I was eleven years old and travelled to North Africa with my parents. We sat on large opulent cushions in a heavily curtained room. No utensils were provided so, to my childish delight, we used our hands. My parents explained to me the importance of using the right hand only, as the role of the left hand in this culture was used for "cleaning up." (If you're a leftie you're going to need to adapt.)

I still love making couscous. Couscous is simple, quick, and easy to prepare whilst also being tasty and healthy. It's great on its own or with vegetables, lamb, chicken, fish—anything goes. Simon loves it as a sweet dish and sprinkles his couscous with almonds, cinnamon, and sugar.

We arrived in Morocco during Ramadan, a religious holiday that forbids eating and drinking between sunup and sundown. It was late 2003, and we had just begun of our trip, having been on the road for only six months. We eased our way gently into this foreign culture and continent, our destination the Erg Chebbi. The Erg Chebbi is one of Morocco's two Saharan ergs, massive seas of dunes formed by windblown sand. We spent a few weeks here sand training before crossing the Sahara Desert itself.

Camping for a few weeks in the grounds of a small Au Berge (Moroccan Guest House), we ate more couscous than I ever thought possible. But rather than putting me off, I was hooked. Today, I always try to carry a small bag of couscous with us, wherever we are in the world.

Most Western supermarkets sell pre-steamed and dried couscous, which is quick and easy, ready in around five minutes. I add fruits and nuts and usually eat it as a side to meat or poultry.

# COUSCOUS

## ingredients

- » 4 tbsp. slivered almonds
- » 4 tbsp. olive oil
- » 1 red pepper cut into small pieces
- » ½ red onion, cut into wedges and separated
- » 1 small green chilli, finely chopped (optional)
- » 1 clove garlic, minced
- » 2 tbsp. lime juice or lemon juice
- » ¼ tsp. ground cinnamon
- » 1 tsp. ground coriander
- » 1 tsp. ground cumin
- » 1 cup (8oz/230g) quick-cooking couscous
- » 4 tbsp. raisins
- » 1¼ cups (300 ml) chicken or vegetable stock
- » 1 tbsp. finely chopped fresh cilantro (1 tsp. mixed dry herbs is an okay alternative.)

## method

1. Lightly toast the almonds in a dry frying pan until golden brown. Remove from the pan and set aside.

2. Heat 1 tablespoon of the olive oil in the frying pan. Add the red pepper, red onion, and chilli (optional) and stir-fry for 5 minutes.

3. Remove and place to one side.

4. Place the remaining 3 tablespoons of olive oil, garlic, lime juice, cinnamon, coriander, and cumin in a jar with a screw-top lid and shake to mix. Or, if you don't have a sealed jar, place all the ingredients in a cup and beat together well with a fork.

5. Mix the couscous with the raisins (and if you are using dried herbs, also add them now) in your saucepan (or large non-plastic bowl) and pour the boiling stock over the mix. Use less water than you think you need, rather than too much, during the mixing stage. Stodgy, watery couscous is awful and it's easier to add a little more but impossible to remove excess water. Properly cooked couscous is smooth, light, and fluffy, not gummy or gritty.

6. Cover to seal in the steam and let sit for 10 minutes.

7. Fluff the couscous with a fork to separate the grains. If it's still a little grainy, then add a couple of tablespoons of hot water and stir in and leave. Repeat if necessary.

8. Stir in the red pepper, red onion, almonds, and cilantro.

9. Pour in the dressing and toss together until well combined.

10. Add shredded chicken or canned tuna.

## variations

1. Cooked sweet potato, pumpkin, zucchini, or eggplant can replace the red pepper.

2. Instead of cilantro use fresh flat-leaf parsley, or mint.

3. Instead of almonds use pistachios, pine nuts, or walnuts.

4. Instead of raisins, use chopped apricots, dates, prunes, sultanas, or dried cranberries.

5. Use spring onions instead of red onion.

6. Add 1 cup canned chickpeas, rinsed and drained.

Prep time: 5 minutes
Cooking time: 15 minutes (including steaming the couscous)
Utensils: frying pan, cup, and 2-litre saucepan

## TIP

Couscous is nice as a side to either BBQ chicken in homemade BBQ sauce (see sauce recipe on page 133) or any kind of cooked meat or poultry. You can serve this dish immediately if you like it warm or leave to cool a little.

SIMON HAS PRODUCED SOME GREAT MEALS OVER THE YEARS BUT THIS IS ONE OF HIS FAVOURITES. HE LIKES IT "CHEAP AND EASY."

NO COMMENTS PLEASE!

LISA THOMAS

# SIMON'S TUNMATO SAUCE

Prep time: 5 minutes
Cooking time: 10 minutes
Utensils: small saucepan

## ingredients

» *1 tbsp. olive oil*

» *1 medium onion, finely chopped*

» *2 garlic cloves, finely chopped*

» *1 small chilli, chopped (optional)*

» *Fresh zucchini (optional)*

» *1 (260g) tin tuna (drained)*

» *3 tbsp. tomato puree*

» *1 heaped tsp. sugar or 1 sachet of sweetener*

» *Ground black pepper*

» *1 large tin (14.5oz/400g) chopped tomatoes or 5 fresh tomatoes, finely chopped*

## method

1. Heat the olive oil in a pan and fry the onion, garlic, chilli (optional), and zucchini (optional) until the garlic is lightly browned.

2. Add the tuna, tomato puree, sugar, and pepper. Mix well and fry for 2 minutes.

3. Add the chopped tomatoes, stir well, and simmer for another 5 minutes. If you are using fresh tomatoes and they are not very juicy, you may need to add 1 or 2 tablespoons of water.

4. Mix sauce into your already-cooked pasta.

# GETTING SAUCY
## IN THE GOBI

THIS IS HOW AN EVENING MEAL WITH
NEW FRIENDS IN MONGOLIA STARTS.
THEY BRING THE MEAT. WE SUPPLY
THE VEGTABLES AND BBQ SAUCE.

I marinate pork chops, pork ribs, and chicken pieces in this tasty BBQ sauce. It's also great for disguising poor quality meat.

Prep time: 2 minutes
Cooking time: 10 minutes
Utensils: zip-top bag

# TASTY BBQ SAUCE

## ingredients

» 1 tsp. mustard

» 1 tbsp. olive oil

» 2½ tbsp. tomato ketchup

» 1½ tbsp. soy sauce

» 4 tbsp. honey

» 1 tbsp. Worcestershire sauce

## method

1. Mix all of the ingredients together in a screw-top jar and shake well. If you don't have a screw-top jar, mix it in a mug with a fork and beat well.

2. Once the mixture is a nice dark brown colour and mixed completely, pour it over meat or poultry.

3. It's best to put your meat into a zip-top bag and pour the sauce in. Ensure you seal the bag and then "squidge" (yep, I've decided that's the correct word) the packet between your fingers so the meat is completely covered with the sauce.

4. Make sure the packet is well sealed and let sit 20 minutes or so before cooking.

# 24| LEMONY SNIKETS

Over the years, I have used this easy but tasty sauce to pep up dull meat. Dipping pieces of chicken or pork into the sauce before skewering and placing onto a barbeque or open fire instantly improves the flavour. Or you can simply use as a baste for barbequing fish.

Preparing this sauce always brings back vivid memories of São Paulo in Brazil where I treated Simon to his favourite rice dish, an Italian risotto. He had just undergone major surgery to stabilize his broken neck, and I was recovering from malaria. (Yet again, and you have to wait for the full story in another book.)

São Paulo is a culturally rich city, so obtaining real Italian risotto was no issue. I cooked it the traditional way, finishing off with this lemon-garlic sauce, two bunches of fresh arugula, and grated parmesan during the final moments of cooking. Along with a carefully chosen bottle of red wine, this meal was our celebration of survival.

Prep time: 3 minutes
Cooking time: 10 minutes
Utensils: sharp knife

I marinate pork chops, pork ribs, and chicken pieces in this tasty BBQ sauce. It's also great for disguising poor quality meat.

# LEMONY-GARLIC SAUCE

## ingredients

» *3 garlic cloves, crushed*

» *1 medium lemon, rind and juice*

» *1 tbsp. water*

» *1 tbsp. olive oil*

» *Handful fresh parsley or coriander, chopped (optional)*

## method

1. In a screw-top jar or coffee mug add crushed garlic, 2 teaspoons of lemon rind (only use the yellow part of the lemon peel because the white part tastes bitter), and 2 tablespoons of juice from the lemon. Shake or mix well.

2. Add this mix to your cooked and drained plain pasta or rice, stirring well, or coat chicken, pork, or fish with the mix during cooking.

# 25 | CARNIVORES ALCHEMY

My mustard glaze adds a little finesse to pork, chicken, or steak. It's also great over cooked potatoes and green beans. This is the perfect glaze to use for either barbequing or cooking in a pan.

---

**FOR SIMON AND ME, GETTING TO KNOW A COUNTRY MEANS WALKING ITS MARKETS.**

---

The markets of Central Asia were like nothing we had ever experienced before with their eclectic variety of produce and immense size. We planned to spend a few hours exploring the fifth largest market in Central Asia in Turkmenistan.

Our hours at the Altyn Asyr bazaar stretched into a whole day of marvelling at all the fresh produce spilling from seller's baskets onto the dirt. The air resounded with the heavy thud of dozens of cleavers hitting chopping boards. In the afternoon sun, we carefully tiptoed around pools of blood collecting at the base of the butchers' tables, each vendor touting stranger cuts of flesh than the one before. No organ was too large or too small and nothing was wasted.

We bartered for a simple cut of almost-recognisable meat. At a nearby fruit seller, we gathered handfuls of sweetly pungent lemons. This was not just a market; this was a city, a vast labyrinth of negotiation. With our purchases made but our sense of direction lost, we pushed and jostled our way through alleyways of tightly packed carpets and brilliantly coloured materials before escaping to the sanctuary of our hostel. Mustard glazed pork was on the menu!

Prep time: 5 minutes
Cooking time: 10 minutes
Utensils: small saucepan

# MUSTARD GLAZE

## ingredients

» *3 tbsp. olive oil*

» *2 tsp. Dijon or whole grain mustard*

» *1 tbsp. lemon juice*

» *1 tsp. finely grated lemon rind*

» *Salt and pepper*

## method

1. In a small bowl, mix together olive oil, mustard, lemon juice, rind, pinch of salt and pepper.

2. Coat your meat with the glaze before cooking.

3. Or add to cooked potatoes and finely sliced onions. Stir in well to ensure the potatoes are nicely coated.

**S**imon has an incredible sweet tooth but, his favourite, which is chocolate, is either not easily available or melts into an impossible mess in our panniers. My baked banana recipe satisfies his sweet cravings. Well, for a short while at least. You can also use plaintains as a side dish prepared this way.

In Kenya, we headed north from Nairobi through a small town called Isiolo on our way to the Samburu Game Reserve. Even though motorcycles are not allowed, we planned to do some bush camping nearby.

We arrived in the small town of Isiolo sooner than anticipated, and so did the throng of vendors who were at our side the moment we stopped for water. Bunches of small sweet bananas were thrust at me to my left, and jewellery and knife vendors were to my right. A couple of guys kicked off an argument about a donkey over my shoulder just for good measure.

The sweet bananas looked too good to resist, and I strapped them to the back of my bike before escaping the chaos.

North of Isiolo, large planks with lethal-looking nails were thrown across the road.

Three guys in army fatigues ushered us into a small wooden shack and instructed us to sign "the book" with our names, country from, country going to and, of course, from which tribe we originated.

Past the plank and nail barriers, the tar road became a very dusty and corrugated track. If we followed this far enough, we would end up in Ethiopia.

By the end of the afternoon, we arrived at the gates of the reserve and found a spot for the tent and bikes, and camped behind some scrub not too far from a borehole. As evening drew in, we threw together a meal of sardine spaghetti, then baked the sweet bananas on the glowing embers on the edges of a roaring fire.

We gorged on bananas covered in honey and sipping locally produced rum whilst being serenaded by a chorus of frogs by a nearby brook.

LISA THOMAS

# BAKED BANANAS
## (A SWEET TREAT OR A SIDE DISH)

## ingredients

» 2 ripe bananas or very ripe plantains (The skin of the plantain should be almost entirely black when it is mature and ready to use.)

» 1 tbsp. honey and some cinnamon if using as a dessert

## method

1. Individually wrap the bananas or plantains, skins on, in aluminium foil. Alternately, place them, with their skins on, in a covered pot. Using a pot helps retain the juices in the same way as using aluminium foil.

2. Place the foil-wrapped fruit (or the pot) on a rack above hot burning embers of the fire—not directly over the flames.

3. Bake for 10–15 minutes for bananas or 20–25 minutes for plantains. The sweet smell of the sugars will let you know when they are done.

4. Carefully open up the foil. Make a slit down the middle of the skin and open up the banana or plantain.

5. If using as a dessert, drizzle with honey and dust with cinnamon or use sweetened condensed milk instead. If using as a side dish, leave the plantains in their natural juices and place on top of white rice as a side to your main meat dish.

6. These are best served eaten directly from their skins with a spoon.

LISA THOMAS
······

# ACKNOWLEDGMENTS

Every week for three months I sent the same recipe to a select group of testers and awaited the comments. They were from very different pathways in life: the corporate world, a teacher, a traveller, a mother, and a chef. They returned their results and thoughts about each recipe, laying out any issues they had with my isntructions. They all promised me that they had followed them strictly.

I must admit I was a little apprehensive that they would hate some of the meals, and that their families would refuse to eat them. However, they loved the meals, found the recipes easy to follow, and the families even asked for them again.

Jacqui is not the biggest fan of corned beef but enthusiastically reported that everyone "thoroughly enjoyed it!" Lynette told me that she had never managed to cook rice properly but now uses my method as "it produces perfect rice every time."

Other comments of "easy to follow instructions"; "It's great to have different ideas for meals when travelling without having to rack my brain" and, "surprisingly tasty!" have confirmed for me that writing this cookbook has indeed been worth all the pain and pleasure.

I hope that you, too, will enjoy cooking these meals. And I hope that my memories and experiences, each tied so strongly with the recipes, have taken you on a short journey with each meal.

Thank you, Jacqui, Amie, Luanna, Lynette, Sandy, and Lisa. And thank you, Simon, who is not only a wonderful husband but my photographer, designer, taster, and all-round verbal punching bag for when things go wrong.

# LIKE OUR IMAGES?

After exploring and photographing our planet for fourteen years, we have a vast library of award-winning images ready to ship to your door, framed or unframed.

Adventure ☐   Landscape ☐   Portraits ☐   Wildlife ☐   Nature ☐

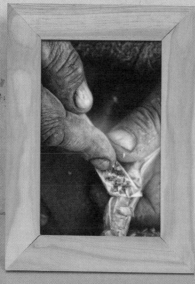

nomad FOTOS

HOME OR
WORKSPACE

## TESTIMONIALS

*I wanted to reach out to thank you for your visit to adidas Head Office. Our entire team was very excited to hear about your adventures and how your experience could apply to innovation and problem solving across our global platform. Your presentation was lively, funny, and informative and above all, inspiring.*
Sr. Director, adidas

*Simon and Lisa captured the audience's attention immediately and delivered, with high energy and enthusiasm, to a full house. I would happily recommend Simon and Lisa Thomas (aka 2 Ride the World) to any Company or Organisation looking to motivate and inspire their Staff with something a little different that encourages the audience to set and achieve their own life goals.*
Andrew,
Mortgage & Finance Association of Australia

*Lisa & Simon stand out as an audience captivating team. They definitely belong to the thin upper league of real world travellers and presenters who can be trusted to present anywhere for any audience.*
Kimmo, Touratech-USA

*Over the last twelve years we have had the pleasure of hosting some 100-plus presentations from both regular and BIG name adventure moto-personalities alike. It's easy to say that Lisa and Simon set a new standard by which all future presenters will be measured. With almost 160 guests the turnout was close to store capacity!*
Brendan, GM SOUTH SOUND MOTORCYCLES

# CONNECT WITH US

We have been travelling continuously since 2003 and share our stories and photographs via our website and on the various social media sites. We also speak at industry events around the globe. We'd love to connect with you via our email newsletter, in person, or on your favourite online hangout. So, drop by and say hi.

 facebook/2RideTheWorld

 instagram/2RideTheWorld

 twitter/2RideTheWorld

 plus.google/2RideTheWorld

 youtube/2RideTheWorld

 email: lisathomas@2ridetheworld.com

 2RIDETHEWORLD.COM

# JOIN US ON A RIDE

Would you like to travel with us on a short or longer motorcycle expedition? Drop by the website or sign up for the newsletter online and be the first to hear about opportunities to join the journey.

"Hey Lisa,
What an incredible trip.
Thanks for an amazing experience."
Client: Eric Uber

# 2RIDETHEWORLD.COM

# INDEX

# NOTES

# NOTES